RESTORING the PUBLIC TRUST

A Fresh Vision
for Progressive Government
in America

Peter G. Brown

BEACON PRESS / BOSTON

BEACON PRESS
25 Beacon Street
Boston, Massachusetts 02108-2892

Beacon Press books
are published under the auspices of
the Unitarian Universalist Association of Congregations.

Excerpts from Milton Friedman, *Capitalism and Freedom,*
© 1962, 1982 by the University of Chicago,
used by permission of the University of Chicago Press
and the author.

99 98 97 96 95 94   8 7 6 5 4 3 2 1

Text design by Daniel Ochsner

Library of Congress Cataloging-in-Publication Data

Brown, Peter G.
Restoring the public trust : a fresh vision for progressive
government in America / Peter G. Brown.
p.   cm.
Includes bibliographical references and index.
ISBN 0-8070-4306-0
1. Legitimacy of governments—United States. 2. Political
planning—United States. 3. Political participation—United States.
4. United States—Politics and government. I. Title.
JK271.B667   1991
323'.04'0973—dc20   93-7089
CIP

The ideas of economists and political philosophers, both when they are right and when they are wrong, are more powerful than is commonly understood. Indeed the world is ruled by little else. Practical men, who believe themselves to be quite exempt from any intellectual influences, are usually the slaves of some defunct economist. Madmen in authority, who hear voices in the air, are distilling their frenzy from some academic scribbler a few years back. . . . Soon or late, it is ideas, not vested interests, which are dangerous for good or evil.

JOHN MAYNARD KEYNES, *The General Theory*
of Employment, Interest and Money

There is nothing wrong with the United States that a dose of smaller and less intrusive government would not cure.

MILTON FRIEDMAN, October 1983

All power is a trust; . . . we are accountable for its exercise; that, from the people, and for the people all springs, and all must exist.

BENJAMIN DISRAELI, *Vivian Grey*

Contents

Acknowledgments

Dan Yankelovich helped focus my thinking in the mid-1980s by asking for a "new framework" for government. Peter Shepherd grasped the importance of rediscovering the foundations of political legitimacy and gave more than generously of his encouragement, time, ideas, and thoughtful questioning. As my criticisms of the market model of government legitimacy developed over the years, David Weimer never ceased to prod me to set out a better alternative. Worth Bateman responded to too many successive drafts with insight and patience. Andy Hrycyna of Beacon Press offered key philosophical insights in strengthening the final drafts. Florentin Krause gave generously of his time in discussing the effects of carbon and fuel taxes. Steve Block, Ethan Brown, David Cohen, Robert Fullinwider, Neva Goodwin, Clive Hamilton, Michael Higgins, Fisher Howe, Steve Kelman, Will Marshall, David Mitchell, Bill Moomaw, Frank Muller, Conway Smith, Rob Sprinkle, and Stephen Viederman offered helpful suggestions. Richard Ashcraft, Herman Daly, Richard Elmore, Gelson Fonseca, Hank Jenkins-Smith, Tom Schelling, Henry Shue, and Edith Brown Weiss checked many of the key arguments. The Ethics and Value Studies program of the National Science Foundation provided release time for the development of the trust model in part II. My wife, Judy Brown, put up with thousands of hours of my labor, helped clarify many convoluted sentences, and provided the emotional support for the effort. Gilbert and Mary Wilhelm helped deepen my understanding of stewardship. Defects remain my own.

Linda Ball patiently assisted me in getting the manuscript in final form. I have learned so much from so many of my students at the School of Public Affairs at the University of Maryland that I could not name them all. Those who were of special help are Beth Granata, Ruth Heikkinen, John Hausoul, David Rodgers, Amanda Wolf, and Steve Wooley. I am especially grateful to Associate Dean William Powers and Dean Michael Nacht for allowing me the flexibility to work on this book, to our financial officer Eric Munz for putting up with numerous requests, and to the University of Maryland for all it has given me all these many years.

School of Public Affairs
University of Maryland
College Park, Maryland
January 1993

PETER G. BROWN

We are in the midst of a crisis of governmental legitimacy, of public faith in government. For years our candidates for president have run against Washington, fearing that being identified with government will doom their chances with the electorate. Property tax revolts have become widespread, and incumbents have been swept from office at all levels. Many of us have given up even on the prospect of a "vision" and "philosophy" of government. Just get rid of the corruption and waste, we say to our elected officials, and try to do as little harm as possible. Why do so many people rightly believe that government is not working, that government has betrayed their trust? Certainly part of the answer is twelve years of Reagan/Bush administration efforts to slash government in the name of the free market. I will argue that the conservative program of free market economics is even more radical and mistaken than even opponents often assume. It does not just argue for smaller government; it misunderstands and undermines the bases of political language and political life. But that is not the whole story. Democrats and other liberals have in recent history failed to offer an alternative, broad conception of government that has the power to refute the falsely appealing rhetoric of the Right and lead us to a coherent program of policies that will restore public trust. We are in vital need of a fresh political vocabulary.

The feeling that people have of having had their *trust* betrayed by government is not an accidental feature of this political crisis. I believe that this sense of betrayal should be understood literally. That the relation between a government and its citizens is one of trust is the basic idea underlying a powerful way of rethinking public policy. Seeing government leaders as trustees and citizens as beneficiaries is a simple picture with complex and detailed consequences. A trust conception of govenment offers theoretical virtues that show specifically what is wrong with traditional approaches to public policy, not only on the Right, but in the centrist mainstream of liberal welfare state economics as well. The conception offers a revitalized framework for all of us to think about public responsibilities. And it points to a specific agenda for political action.

Part I of this book looks at the crisis in our theory of governance. The ideas of the free market Right, exemplified in the ideas of Milton Friedman, represent the extreme of an approach that puts the market at the center of a philosophy of government. But that misplaced faith in the market motivates a very wide range of approaches to policy—in the center and even in liberal think tanks like the Brookings Institution. *Restoring the Public Trust* discusses market-based schools of policy theory in depth because the strengths of the trust conception—which aims to put the market in its proper moral place—are best understood in contrast.

Another reason for spending time on the mistakes of the dominant schools of policy thinking in recent decades is that there are trends at work in American political life that even a presidential election cannot overturn by itself. Public disillusionment runs deep, and the forces that brought us to where we are have long histories. Discussions on all sides have been infected by flawed approaches, and policy analysts at think tanks and schools of public policy do not change their jobs when cabinet members do. We need to see clearly the need for redirection. And we need a unified set of "big" ideas to provide a framework for action.

Restoring the Public Trust provides those ideas, setting out in part II the trust conception and its policy implications. The book is addressed to a broad spectrum of readers who are concerned with public issues. One great strength of the trust conception is that it shows a *unified* rationale for a wide range of progressive programs—from health insurance to environmental protection—providing a way for people with various political interests to see themselves as allied in a common vision of government and a shared view of why we should willingly bear the burdens of public life. The book is also aimed at politicians and citizens who are looking for a positive vision of public life and public service after so many years of antigovernment rhetoric and loss of faith. It is my hope that the trust conception can contribute—as ideas can—to actual change, to a renewal of hopeful life and effective government.

Part I

LOSS OF FAITH
IN GOVERNMENT
AND THE CRISIS
IN POLITICAL THEORY

The real battle will be between those who have done their homework and are ready with imaginative ideas, and those who try to hide their intellectual poverty behind a facade of once-fashionable liberal cliches. But the cliches of liberalism are stale: they have lost their power to motivate and inspire: they have also lost their power to govern.

EDWIN J. FEULNER, JR., in the foreword to *Mandate for Leadership*

Chapter 1

THE SOURCES
OF DISILLUSION

The intellectual debate has been framed in our terms.

EDWIN J. FEULNER, JR., in the foreword to
Mandate for Leadership III

It is no coincidence that a crisis of public faith in government coincided with the end of the Reagan/Bush administrations, embodying as they did ideas that denigrated government. These administrations pursued policies that actively dismantled effective government programs, condemning on ideological grounds any government role at all in providing certain forms of public service employment, legal services to the poor, and public transit programs like Conrail. They reduced both the federal role in public housing and benefits to individuals. Under administration proposals, fewer people were eligible for assistance, and those who were saw unemployment benefits reduced, income support limited, and school lunch programs cut back.[1] The Reagan administration also attempted massive cuts in social security.[2]

Nevertheless, when they came to power, those administrations were enormously popular across a wide range of the electorate, and liberal politicians were not seen as offering an alternative vision. Why did voters install administrations that led eventually to such disillusionment? A bit of history is in order.

THE RISE OF THE RIGHT

There are at least two conventional accounts of how a philosophy centered around the idea that a free market should be the centerpiece of public policy came to play a pivotal role in the 1980s. The account emphasized by conservatives focuses on the macrohistorical events of the 1970s. Jimmy Carter, the last nominally liberal president, so this story goes, simply did not have the policy tools at his disposal to deal with the nation's problems. The old liberal framework dating back to Franklin Roosevelt was reaching the end of its useful life. Supply-side economics—the idea that to achieve economic growth we should concentrate on stimulating capital investment rather than consumer demand—appeared to fit nicely with the underlying rationale of a capitalist-oriented minimal state. A vast tax cut could serve as a necessary antidote to the problems of unemployment and inflation by increasing savings and productivity. The predicted surge in economic activity would fund a defense buildup that was taken to be an essential response to the Soviets and increase our ability to respond to brushfire wars around the world. Events convinced people that conservative solutions were called for.

The second account emphasizes the personal charm of Ronald Reagan, the hero of Hollywood Westerns that glorify a golden age, a tall, handsome, uncomplicated man from the Golden State. George Bush carried on the Reagan legacy, combining the halo of Reagan's anointed successor with clever market-oriented campaign tactics. According to this account, it was not the conservative ideology that was decisive, but personalities and tactics. Liberals find this account congenial because it does not threaten the idea that the nation is still fundamentally liberal and because it does not highlight the failures of their own policies and their lack of a coherent political philosophy.

There is something to both these explanations of the failure of liberalism and the success of the Right. But, if we limit our analysis to the surface of these narratives, we miss the deeper structure and meaning of these events. To understand how our political vocabulary has come to be structured and impoverished, we need to set these subplots in the context of broader intellectual and historical trends. The election of Governor Clinton has by no means fully reversed these trends.

The intellectuals who have helped create and influence public policy over the past several decades have embraced and reinforced misleading doctrines about social science and the relations between policy and values. It is these doctrines that assured a vacuum into which the ideas of the Right were able to move and that continue to hamper the Democratic party in articulating a philosophy of governance. The Right's ability to influence, and even control, the intellectual agenda that shapes public policy is a story of victory by default, a story of inaction and narrow horizons on the part of the Left, inaction that has surely contributed to public apathy toward national politics. This is a default that is driven, as we shall see, by misleading ideas central to the very disciplines from which one would have expected sustained criticism—liberal social science that focuses on public policy and liberal political philosophy.

VICTORY BY DEFAULT

It is hard to imagine that even his most committed friends would accuse Ronald Reagan of a scholarly bent. Yet, by the time he took office, he had a full-blown intellectual agenda—built by scholars—for a sweeping reform of the government. That agenda was well worked out, well articulated, and fully detailed—the brainchild of a handful of individuals who set out to change the terms in which public policy was debated. One of those individuals was Joseph Coors, who in 1973 established the Heritage Foundation, the self-described "Washington based . . . public policy research institution dedicated to the principles of free competitive enterprise, limited government, individual liberty and a strong national defense."[3] According to Sidney Blumenthal, "Heritage was begun with a $250,000 grant from Colorado Brewer Joseph Coors. . . . Heritage counts on new money, mostly from the Sunbelt. The self-made men, who view themselves as rugged individuals on an economic frontier . . . view the Liberal Establishment as a foreign, occupying power."[4] It was the Heritage Foundation that in 1981 published *Mandate for Leadership*, a comprehensive conservative agenda for the new administration.

As Gregg Easterbrook reports, Coors was one of a small group:

"The whole transformation of conservative philosophy was really begun by just a handful of people," Michael Horowitz says, and he names Richard Larry, the grant director of the Sarah Scaife Foundation; Michael Joyce, the grant director for the Olin Foundation; and Leslie Lenkowsky, who once controlled grants for the Smith Richardson Foundation.[5]

Horowitz, a former liberal who underwent an intense conversion to the Right, was the general counsel of the Office of Management and Budget early in the Reagan years. A lawyer himself, Horowitz was one of those who spearheaded the attempt to undercut the Legal Services Corporation. Scaife, Coors, and the Olin and Smith Richardson foundations are all substantial donors to the Heritage Foundation.

A noteworthy feature of the Heritage Foundation is its overtly ideological character. It self-consciously set out to support a right-wing view of the world and to develop a political agenda to fit that view. Burton Pines, a

---

vice-president at Heritage, has frankly admitted this political mission: "We're not here to be some kind of Ph.D. committee giving equal time. Our role is to provide conservative public-policy makers with arguments to bolster our side."[6] Heritage is a starker version of the nominally more mainstream American Enterprise Institute (whose swerve from the Right toward the political center nearly brought about its extinction). Organizations like the American Enterprise Institute, Heritage, and the Cato and Hoover institutes have been able to formulate a value-based foundation of ideas for public policy that resonates deeply to our circumstances and history.[7] Those ideas speak to, and apparently fill, the deep hunger of many people for clear-cut notions of right and wrong. They provide a political philosophy from which one can take one's bearings, a philosophy that tells us a story about where we came from and where we should be going. As Easterbrook notes,

> Perhaps the most lasting contribution of the new think tanks is that they have transformed the terms of the public-policy debate. In politics, words are map coordinates that show on whose territory a battle is being fought. Whenever liberalism succeeded in defining its goals as the public interest, in opposition to private interest, victory was near. To the extent that conservatism can now define its goals in terms of the greater good, it can win on merit what it could once win only by quantity of campaign contributions.[8]

The map provided by these institutions is a combination of market-oriented thought, derived from academics like Milton Friedman, and social conservatism, much of which finds its home in religious fundamentalism. The free market advocates see the modern state as interfering with properly operating markets. The religious Right sees the state—or the *liberal* state, at any rate—as illegitimately affecting moral choice: inappropriately allowing choice in such matters as (legal) abortions and pornography and limiting choice in such matters as school prayer.[9] This coalition of free market and religious conservatives is an uneasy alliance: the libertarian ideas of free market advocates can be at odds with social conservatives' demands for state action on issues like abortion and school prayer. But the social conservatives invariably turn to free market economists for guidance on large-scale questions of how the government should approach the economy and social programs, and it is market theorists who dominate thinking about policy on the Right.

As the cold war came to an end in the late 1980s and the centrally planned economies unraveled in the early 1990s, these conservative think tanks were ready to engage in exporting their ideas around the globe. For example, in September 1990, the Cato Institute, along with various Soviet institutions, sponsored a conference called "Transition to Freedom: The New Soviet Challenge" in Moscow.[10] At the conference, Cato president Edward H. Crane echoed the now familiar themes: "When looking to the west you must reject those who promote democratic socialism, . . . or even the so-called mixed economy of the United States. Yours is a unique opportunity to reject all forms of statism, whether in its most pernicious form, communism, or in its more insidious form, the mixed economy."[11]

While the Right was investing millions of dollars in articulating a philosophically coherent approach to policy—and spelling out *and selling* the programs that followed from it—the Left was making no comparable effort. One reason that liberals failed to respond to what turned out to be a real threat was political complacency. They did not rally because they thought they had won: they saw problems with the liberal agenda as failures of technique. If a housing program was not working, it was just that it had not been tinkered with enough. You only had to try hard enough. And, as long as you kept trying, you would be rewarded with office. Investing in theory was not necessary. Frank Thomas, for example, who took over as president of the trend-setting, historically liberal Ford Foundation in 1979, and who had successfully run the effort to revitalize the Bedford Stuyvesant section of Brooklyn, explicitly turned away from an emphasis on social science research and toward action. The foundation withdrew or reduced its support for projects like computer models of the economy and detailed analysis of the costs of transportation systems and concentrated instead on efforts that would demonstrably help the poor. Disillusioned with the excessive promises of social scientists and theorists, Thomas wanted to concentrate on things that worked. We knew, it seemed, how the world should be—the problem was just getting there.

This self-confidence is not difficult to understand. The liberal agenda set forth in the 1960s by Kennedy and Johnson had remained relatively undisturbed during the Nixon and Ford presidencies. Carter seemed to reaffirm the basic message. No investigation of an alternative underlying, organizing, and legitimating ideology seemed necessary since there was little substantial disagreement within the liberal establishment about the fundamental direction that policy should take. The result was that the political activities and doctrines of the Right and their popularity with the nation's voters were largely ignored by the Left.

But forces other than political inattention were at work, too. Liberal intellectuals themselves had given up on the job of providing an overarching, but concrete, political vision. This is not to say that there were not many liberal thinkers working on problems of public policy. By around 1985, the roster of nominally left-oriented think tanks had expanded considerably. In the early 1980s, new organizations with a moderate to liberal orientation had emerged in Washington, D.C.: the Center on National Policy, the Roosevelt Center, the Policy Exchange, and the Economic Policy Institute. Others grew up in New York and on the West Coast, all of them less dominated by economics than the older institutions like Brookings, although they were still staffed by professional social scientists. As Robert Kuttner noted in 1985, "To judge by the recent proliferation of think tanks, institutes and policy councils, the Democratic Party is ablaze with thought."[12]

Even this frenzy of activity, however, led to virtually no progress in solving the problem of providing an overall framework for setting the direction of policy. No political philosophy was produced or even referred to. As Kuttner wrote,

> The liberal quest for serviceable ideas is a little like the old story of the small boy in the barn, sifting through the manure heap, mumbling, "There must be a pony here somewhere." You have to begin with the pony. . . .
>
> The Democrats . . . used to have a few big ideas: the free market couldn't do everything. The state was a very useful counterweight to the market. The little guy deserved more breaks than the marketplace often delivered. And the Democrats had a lot of particular policy approaches informed by that one conviction. Most Democrats still think they are the party of the little guy, but they are no longer quite sure what to think about the state and the market.
>
> In this ideological vacuum, the idea of "new ideas" for the sake of new ideas serves as a convenient stand in for the coherent worldview the Democrats no longer have.[13]

What went wrong? How could we have spent so much—and worked so hard—but come up with so little?

The people who work for such organizations as Brookings, the Urban Institute, and Resources for the Future, on which the proliferating liberal think tanks were modeled, have a certain understanding of what proper research looks like. Dominated by the canons of economics and political science, research within these institutions must be "objective," and to be acceptably objective means to be value free. Where the Heritage Foundation supports research to underpin policies that will enhance individual liberty, the new and the old liberal think tanks in the tradition of Brookings insist that objective reports must avoid value judgments.[14] Since the question of what values we ought to hold is deemed beyond the purview of legitimate inquiry, institutions in the Brookings tradition have a lot to say about means, but not much about ends. Their fundamental and mistaken assumption about values undercuts their contribution since policy is unavoidably about what we ought to do.

Why do the social scientists in liberal policy organizations refuse to consider, argue for, and defend the values that are inherent in policy? Why do they insist on this understanding of objectivity? The answer derives from several mutually reinforcing sources.

The first source is the intellectual tradition in which public policy research grew up. The Brookings Institution was founded in 1927 at the instigation of Robert S. Brookings, a businessman, by a merger of two preexisting institutions, to advise the government about matters of public policy.[15] Brookings was concerned that effective governance increasingly involved the ability to understand and control the economy and therefore could be achieved only with accurate information. According to Donald Critchlow,

> The origins of the Brookings Institution are found in a movement by a self-designated "better element" who persistently disclaimed democracy and party spirit. This element, under the guise of progressive reform and efficient government, consciously sought to weaken partisan interests in public policy and shift decision making as much as possible from elected officials to appointed bodies.
>
> . . . Seeing themselves standing above partisan politics, by operating outside the political arena, yet formulating and passing judgment on public issues, the staff of the Brookings Institution perceived themselves as a professional elite, the guardians of the Republic.[16]

Brookings was founded in the salad days of the public administration movement. As the name of the movement suggests, public administration was concerned with the logistics of carrying out government programs. The logic of the discipline depended on a hard distinction between facts and values. Values were the domain of the legislative body, or elected officials generally, and administrators were involved with carrying out instructions, not with setting a value-based agenda.[17] Interestingly, what role explicitly value-laden issues would play surfaced early and in the person of Brookings himself. A profound difference arose between Brookings, as founder, and the institute's first president, economist Harold G. Moulton. Critchlow reports that, in 1932, "Brookings wrote to Moulton imploring him to have the institution address the problems of inequality in the current system." But the founder was not to prevail. A crippling orthodoxy had already established itself:

> The founder's vision was narrowed by the social scientists, who were less interested than he in reform per se and placed their confidence instead in the ability of the marketplace to ultimately adjust economic and social ills. Brookings, the capitalist, proved to be much more inclined to question the status quo than did experts who prided themselves on their objectivity.[18]

As for a second source, the denigration of values suggests that, probably unknowingly, policy intellectuals within the mainstream have embraced the "emotive theory of values" defended in the 1920s by the linguistic philosopher A. J. Ayer.[19] From the perspective of this theory, statements such as "Murder is wrong" are merely expressions of the emotions of the utterer. They are not statements that can be true or false about the world, making "objectivity" about values impossible. This theory has long since been universally rejected by philosophers, including Ayer himself. But, given the compartmentalization of academic disciplines in the United States, this rejection would likely be startling news to many mainstream social scientists. Whatever its philosophical underpinnings, the emotion-based understanding of value screens out the kind of research that must be undertaken if the Left is to formulate a coherent alternative to the value-based program of the Right.

A third factor contributing to the values vacuum is the insecurity of the social sciences. The physical sciences and biological sciences have an enviable rigor. They explain a great deal, and their predictions are remarkably accurate. Social scientific explanations, on the other hand, are limited, often seeming only to redescribe the events for which one is seeking an explanation. The predictions of even the most robust of the social sciences—economics—are notoriously uncertain, and all but the most die-hard economists have softened claims about being able to fine-tune the economy. Many social scientists have reacted to these disciplinary limitations by trying to emulate the physical sciences. Questions of value are seen as contentious and subjective. The only path to rigor, it is believed, is to concentrate on falsifiable matters of fact, preferably facts that are quantifiable.

This emphasis on quantifiability has had an important indirect effect on our political agenda and is related to a fourth tendency that makes a critique of the Right by liberal social scientists difficult. Of the policy-relevant social sciences, the one that is most amenable to numerical techniques is economics. Because of the intellectual challenge of the discipline, and because of its greater predictive powers, economics has achieved a privileged position among the social sciences. The real "pros" at many think tanks are the numerically sophisticated economists. They see the policy problems of the world through the lens of their discipline, and that means that they take the market as their fundamental point of departure for thinking about public policy. As a consequence, whatever their personal values may be, they have a disciplinary orientation that makes it especially difficult to mount criticisms of the free market philosophy of the Right. The conceptual tools provided by their education and by their profession simply do not suggest an alternative perspective. That the commitment to the market framework is itself founded on a set of incomplete and tacitly assumed values is simply not acknowledged by most researchers.

Economics blocks the development of moral argument about what public policy should be in another way, through its emphasis on the role of self-interest in human motivation. Many economists deny the very idea of *the public interest*, seeing the use of the term as merely a cover for private interests. They cut themselves off from any grounds on which to oppose private interests except other private interests. That private interests do in fact masquerade as public interests is true, but this does not alter the nihilistic consequences of denying that the concept *the public interest* has meaning.[20]

Fifth, and ironically, this understanding of *objectivity* and its emphasis on quantifiability is reinforced by a value commitment inherent in a liberal orientation, a commitment to tolerance. Values (other than tolerance itself, which is taken as exempt from the relativism of other values) are personal and private, to be protected from public intrusion. The state may not legitimately interfere with sexual preference, religious beliefs, leisure time, or one's sense of fairness. Within a liberal social science framework of tolerance, this protection of privacy and diversity is generalized to a global conclusion that no matters of value are the proper domain of public attention and public policy. Thus, it is thought that, even if discussing them were not scientifically irrelevant, there is sufficient *moral* reason to leave values outside the purview of policy discussion.

The result of all this is that, despite the vast amount of money spent by think tanks and the large numbers of talented people employed in them, the liberal and centrist institutions have by and large been crippled in setting out an adequate framework for public policy. Denying themselves the language of values, these institutions have failed to counter the rise of the Right by providing an alternative account of the relation between the state and the market. As Robert Kuttner writes,

> If policy-wonks a political program made, the Democrats would be home free. Washington is full of the species. . . . The . . . older generation of quasi-acadmic outfits such as Brookings and the Urban Institute . . . are even further removed . . . from breathing some life back into the Democratic Party and American liberalism [than their newer counterparts]. The trouble is that few of these [older think tanks] think of policy as something connected to politics. What strikes me over and over again . . . is their political innocence. The assumption is that technicians will put the world right.[21]

Looking outside the social sciences for alternatives to, and criticisms of, the Right, it might seem natural to turn to the discipline of philosophy—a field that concerns itself with questions of meaning, obligation, and the role and nature of the state. The contemporary pickings here, too, are, however, surprisingly thin. Only a handful of books on the philosophical aspects of policy have appeared in recent years from liberals, most notably John Rawls's *A Theory of Justice.*[22] But a book here and there, even one as sweeping and widely read as Rawls's, does not serve to counter the philosophical flood from the Right. Why do liberal academic philosophers make so few attempts to articulate a contemporary political philosophy, and why are those that are attempted regarded as arcane by those involved in setting policy?

Philosophers are widely perceived to have little or nothing to contribute to the debate about public policy because of the standards they hold for *themselves.* In our century, philosophy has, like the social sciences, undergone a crisis of identity. Although philosophers debate about what it is exactly that as philosophers they do, a common understanding has been that, whatever philosophy is, it is different in kind from science. What scientists do par excellence is investigate and explain the real world. Leaving science to the scientists, philosophers see their job as clarifying concepts, not investigating facts. Once the canons of acceptable research within philosophy get defined in this way, the prospects of philosophers having much to say about public policy drops to near zero.[23] Philosophical writing is generally abstract and self-referential. Even in social and political philosophy, where one would hope to find some guidance on practical affairs, debate is typically removed from real policy and real politics. Thinking about public policy issues involves addressing a host of factual questions: the history of problems and programs, the social realities creating demand for services, the number of people in need of services, etc. In a word, you need to be willing to talk a lot about the world and about the conceptual frameworks, arguments, and findings of other disciplines. It is no accident that philosophers who have had the greatest effect on the terms of public debate—people like Daniel Callahan of the Hastings Center, Michael Novak of the American Enterprise Institute, and Michael Walzer of the Institute for Advanced Study—have chosen to pursue careers largely outside the realm of conventional academic philosophy.

Philosophers' refusal to talk about facts when they discuss values, together with mainstream social scientists' refusal to talk about values when they discuss facts, leaves an empty intellectual stage on which the ideas of the Right were able to attain dominance.

After the disastrous 1988 election, of course, Democrats regrouped. Organizations such as the Progressive Policy Institute drew together teams of experts, but this time less wedded to the orthodoxies of traditional social science. They provided the party's presidential candidate with an array of new and attractive ideas in areas as diverse as defense, children and families, education, and the economy. And, given popular disillusionment and an unhealthy economy, they won. But still, an organizing vision, a ground for the legitimacy of government, a conception of a good society, and a sound and humane foreign policy eluded their grasp.[24] That vision, however, was near to hand. In the early part of the campaign, Bill Clinton and Al Gore stressed the idea of a new covenant, "a solemn agreement between the people and their government, based not simply on what each of us can take but on what all of us must give to our nation."[25] In *Earth in the Balance,* Gore relied heavily on the important concept of stewardship in grounding his policy proposals concerning the environment.[26] But Gore did not extend his inquiry to a general theory of legitimacy. Despite a sweeping victory on election day, the new administration was without a philosophy of governance.

The trust model that I set out in part II of this book is meant, in part, to fill that gap. But it is essential first to look in detail at the trust conception's competitors among approaches to public policy. Having been so prominently influential for so long, the doctrines of the free market Right have to be thoroughly displayed and discredited. And, if liberals themselves are to be convinced of the need for a new vision, we need to see clearly, too, the failures of the more centrist version of the role of government typically held by researchers at think tanks like Brookings and the Urban Institute. Indeed, it is these centrist versions with their fascination with the market, and their simultaneous but strongly inconsistent assumption that research must be value free, that set the stage, in part, for the Right's mistakes and in this way contributed, albeit unintentionally and unknowingly, to the rise of dysfunctional government in the United States.

Chapter 2

JUSTIFYING THE CONSERVATIVE REVOLUTION

Ronald Reagan was to say that *Mandate* gave him and his Administration "special substantive help we'll never forget. . . . We've been using *Mandate* to our and the country's advantage." By the end of the President's first year in office, nearly two-thirds of *Mandate's* more than 2000 specific recommendations had been or were being transformed into policy.

> EDWIN J. FEULNER, JR., in the foreword to
> *Mandate for Leadership II*

SUPERB.

> RONALD REAGAN'S endorsement of Milton Friedman's
> *Free to Choose*

Let the rallying cry of the new perestroika be "Free to choose!"

> EDWARD H. CRANE, 1990

As the first Reagan administration began it had in hand the Heritage Foundation's *Mandate for Leadership (Mandate I)*.[1] According to Edwin Feulner, Jr., *Mandate I* had "already had an impact in Washington, due to the pre-publication release of the draft manuscript to President-Elect Reagan's transition team and to the press in November of 1980."[2] A second version, called *Mandate II*, was published as the second Reagan term began.[3] Writing in the *Atlantic*, Gregg Easterbrook noted, "Probably no other documents have been as widely circulated in Washington during the past five years as *Mandate I* and *Mandate II*."[4] *Mandate for Leadership* is a collection of commissioned essays spelling out the policy priorities that follow from a libertarian perspective. It contains a chapter on each of the cabinet departments and major regulatory agencies. Although it is over one thousand pages long, its central message is simple and stark. In the section on the Office of Management and Budget (OMB)—the office that oversees the entire federal budget—the following passage occurs:

> The most difficult job for the President and OMB will be to articulate the policy goals in such a way as to make them useful as a screen for developing more specific program criteria. Without these goals and criteria the budget becomes an amorphous accounting ledger rather than a tool for governing the nation. Unless the philosophy of the President is translated into specific goals and criteria, there can be no basis for allocating the budget aggregates. . . .
>
> Philosophy. The free market, operating as vehicle for millions of individual decisions, is a more efficient allocator of resources than government and leads, therefore, to greater production and higher real income for all workers.
>
> Budget Policy Goal. Limit or eliminate the use of federal funds for programs which interfere with the setting of prices and the allocation of resources by the free market except where the defense of the nation or the public health is endangered.
>
> Program Criteria. Federal programs should conform to the following criteria:
>
> 1. Free market prices must be maintained.
> 2. The rights of individuals to buy and sell goods and services at free market prices must not be abridged.
> 3. The free flow of commodities must be maintained.
> 4. Government purchasing power and credit are not to be used to alter the distribution of goods and services except for purchases and sales required for the functioning of the government.
>
> It will be necessary for the President to develop such a progression from philosophy to program criteria for each major public policy area.[5]

The balance of *Mandate for Leadership* is an elaboration of these ideas with respect to the different policy areas covered by the various departments and regulatory agencies. A key element was tax reform. Another was changing the decision-making process at the OMB. On 17 February 1981, effectively implementing this second goal, President Reagan signed Executive Order 12291, requiring all new major regulations of the federal government to be reviewed by the OMB in accordance with the procedures of cost/benefit analysis. Under this rule, monetary values were assigned to the positive and negative consequences of proposed regulations, and policies would be approved only if the benefits were calculated to exceed the costs.[6]

It would be too simple to say that the Reagan and Bush administrations followed every recommendation contained in this voluminous report. In fact, the further to the Right one is, the more one can regard those administrations as failures for not having gone far enough. But it is fair to say that *Mandate* and its showcasing of the market reflected the underlying framework of Reagan/Bush policy and summarized an approach to policy at the heart of the secular conservative program that dominated political debate in the 1980s and early 1990s. The Right now advocates that the formerly Communist-run Eastern Bloc states adopt this perspective.[7]

The term *market* has two senses that are often run together. In one sense, the looser of the two, the word refers simply to any exchange of one thing for another. If a person who makes spears exchanges them with a hunter for meat, then a market for spears and meat has been created. The more familiar and precise sense of *market* refers to a self-regulating activity where supply and demand are kept in equilibrium through the mechanism of prices. In this latter sense, transactions are part of a much larger system in which prices are determined or heavily influenced by factors beyond the control of the people or firms involved in any given transaction.[8]

The idea is simple. Normally functioning adults buy and sell what they need and want. Theoretically, everyone can play this market game. Someone raises more tomatoes than she needs in her backyard, so she sells them from a roadside stand. The price is set on the basis of competition with other suppliers. The seller gets what she wants—she could not use the tomatoes, but she can use the money. The buyer gets what he wants—he would rather have the tomatoes than the money, as his behavior shows. The firm that builds a television set in Korea that ends up in a living room in New Mexico is engaged in just the same kind of behavior. In both cases, labor and material are exchanged for income. The medium is money.

A market is a "free" market insofar as there is no legal prohibition against transactions. If there is a quota on Korean television sets, then the market is unfree to the degree that purchases that would have occurred do not. If the seller of the tomatoes must have a license to sell them, her liberty is less comprehensive than it otherwise would have been. A completely free market is one in which there are absolutely no legal barriers to the buying and selling of anything, one in which prices are set exclusively by sellers responding to competition. The millions and millions of transactions that occur every day in markets of all sorts are the elements of free market capitalism.

The foundation of free market capitalism is an understanding of liberty as the maximization of individual choice. By placing this concept at the core of its account of state legitimacy, the Right thus makes its position naturally attractive by appealing to a value that has been central to Western culture generally since the Reformation and to American culture since before the Revolution. But what reasons can be offered for believing that these ideas are the proper standards for judging the role of government? Here, although I think that the arguments of the market Right are profoundly mistaken, I set them forth as clearly as I can.

A REPRESENTATIVE OF THE CHICAGO SCHOOL

I focus on Milton Friedman's *Capitalism and Freedom* and *Free to Choose* because Friedman has been the most successful popularizer of the secular ideas of the Right.[9] These works have sold hundreds of thousands of copies, *Free to Choose* has been used as the basis of a television series, and Friedman even possesses academic credibility, having won the Nobel Prize for economics in 1976. Many other people with similar views can be found at the University of Chicago, George Mason University, and the University of California, Los Angeles (sometimes referred to as the University of *Chicago*, Los Angeles). And, of course, there are very influential precursors to Friedman's work, such as Friedrich von Hayek's 1945 *The Road to Serfdom*.[10]

Conservative ideas from the academy have, in turn, served as the frame of reference for the think tanks of the Right, which have set out consciously to reshape the framework for governance in this country. The 1982 *Economic Report of the President* reads like a paraphrase of *Capitalism and Freedom*.[11] The criticisms set forth in the next chapter apply to this whole school of thought, but I have concentrated on one author who is a typical and influential example.

Friedman's basic argument is that the minimum state will produce the best result by preserving the supreme human value: individual liberty. In *Free to Choose*, he finds history on his side: "The story of the United States is the story of an economic miracle and a political miracle that was made possible by the translation into practice of two sets of ideas—both, by a curious coincidence, formulated in documents published in the same year, 1776." One of these documents was Adam Smith's *Wealth of Nations*, the other the Declaration of Independence, written by Thomas Jefferson. According to Friedman, "The combination of economic and political *freedom* produced a golden age in both Great Britain and the United States in the nineteenth century."[12]

Liberty is taken to mean absence of intervention in individual choice by other individuals or institutions. The central good is the maximization of choice. Michael Novak explains it thus: "Each individual human being will have . . . an almost unlimited series of choices about how to spend his or her life."[13] As Isaiah Berlin has pointed out, *liberty* has two different senses.[14] One is positive, a matter of whether individuals have the means to act on their choices. A person is positively free with respect to housing if she has the means to buy appropriate housing. This is freedom *to*. The other conception—that emphasized by the Right—is negative liberty, or liberty *from*.

Negative liberty has both a political and an economic aspect, and both are connected to the market. Liberty to make whatever transaction you want in the marketplace is itself an instance of freedom. The wider the range of items that can be bought and sold, the greater the potential for the exercise of liberty. In the housing market, for instance, one's freedom is enhanced by a wide array of choices. As a consequence of giving consumers freedom to choose, builders have more choice about what to build, laborers more latitude about where to work, lenders more scope in deciding where to put their capital. The situation seems obviously preferable, at least from the perspective of negative liberty, to one in which local zoning is used to restrict housing choices for citizens.

Building a society on this conception of liberty solves, in Friedman's view, a fundamental human problem: "The basic problem of social organization is how to co-ordinate the economic activities of large numbers of people." In Friedman's view, there are a very limited number of ways to do this:

> Fundamentally, there are only two ways of co-ordinating the economic activities of millions. One is central direction involving the use of coercion—the technique of the army and of the modern totalitarian state. The other is voluntary co-operation of individuals—the technique of the market place.
>
> The possibility of co-ordination through voluntary co-operation rests on the elementary—yet frequently denied—proposition that both parties to an economic transaction benefit from it, *provided the transaction is bi-laterally voluntary and informed.*
>
> Exchange can therefore bring about co-ordination without coercion. A working model of a society organized through voluntary exchange is a *free private enterprise exchange economy*—what we have been calling competitive capitalism.[15]

Competitive capitalism organized through markets is thus based on and becomes the most powerful expression of a form of liberty that we can call *market liberty*. Not only does market liberty maximize the range of consumer choice; it is consistent with and reinforces a political system of free citizens.

Market liberty rests on a guiding individualistic metaphor for thinking about society, a metaphor on which more than one member of the Right rely. It is put in especially direct form by Friedman:

> In its simplest form, such a society consists of a number of independent households—a collection of Robinson Crusoes, as it were. Each household uses the resources it controls to produce goods and services that it exchanges for goods and services produced by other households, on terms mutually acceptable to the two parties to the bargain. It is thereby enabled to satisfy its wants indirectly by producing goods for its own immediate use. The incentive for adopting this indirect route is, of course, the increased product made possible by division of labor and specialization of function. Since the household always has the alternative of producing directly for itself, it need not enter into any exchange unless it benefits from it. Hence, no exchange will take place unless both parties do benefit from it. Co-operation is thereby achieved without coercion.[16]

Through voluntary exchange in the market, freedom of choice is enhanced and the problem of coordination solved.

Friedman and fellow free market celebrant Michael Novak, who also addresses this question, have essentially three arguments for the supremacy of market liberty beyond its role in coordinating action. One is that it is a good in itself: "Freedom in economic arrangements is itself a component of freedom broadly understood, so economic freedom is an end in itself."[17] Freedom allows us to do more of what we want, not what others want us to do, and to be who we want to be.

The second argument for market liberty is that economic freedom undergirds political freedom. *Capitalism and Freedom* makes a case for the essential connection between the two: "The kind of economic organization that provides economic freedom directly, namely, competitive capitalism, also promotes political freedom because it separates economic power from political power and in this way enables the one to offset the other."[18] In free competitive markets, power is dispersed. Friedman's argument about the relation between governmental power and economic power is basically an extension of Madison's insight in the *Federalist Papers* (no. 10) about the dispersion of power *within* government to the relation between government and society. The way to prevent the abuse of power is to prevent its concentration.

With economic power dispersed in a capitalist economy, opportunities for *political* dissent will be maximized. Effective disagreement with the state requires financial backing. Pamphlets have to be printed, travel financed, media space and time purchased. Without the means to disseminate ideas, liberty of expression is without practical force. Friedman explicitly argues that, in a market-based society, all dissenters need is access to money, or to people with money whom they can convince of their message, to be able to get the message out, a system that may not be perfect but that is better than the alternative of political tyranny.[19] Even in a democratic socialist society, the task of raising money for dissent is formidable at best, and probably impossible. The government is unlikely to finance an attack on its own policies, and no private citizen will have the resources to do it since socialism does not permit the concentration of wealth. Nor is it likely that small amounts could be raised from many persons to finance political opposition since, if this were possible, the job of convincing them of the dissenting position would already have been accomplished.

Political liberty is secured, not only by decentralized concentrations of wealth, but also by decentralized opportunities for employment: "An impersonal market separates economic activities from political views and protects men from being discriminated against in their economic activities for reasons that are irrelevant to their productivity—whether their reasons are associated with their views or their color."[20] It thus turns out that economic factors are instrumental in, or, in Friedman's terms, a necessary condition of, the exercise of other liberties. As Michael Novak puts it, "An economic order built upon respect for the decisions of the individual in the marketplace, upon rights to property which the state may not abridge; and upon limiting the activities of the central state, are at the very least harmonious with the habits of mind required for a functioning democratic political order."[21]

The third reason for favoring "free" markets is the wealth that they create. Here is what Michael Novak says about efficiency:

> If democratic capitalism has conferred enormous wealth upon the world, a wealth never before even envisaged except in a few places, for a very few, and unsteadily, it has also proven to be the most *efficient* system ever devised by human beings. Whatever its faults—and these are many—no other system even comes close to it in inventiveness, production, and widespread distribution. Socialist systems have proved to be less successful. . . . There are serious flaws in the sort of efficiency generated by democratic capitalism. Unplanned and unguided, our system permits shortages in some areas and unnecessary abundance and wastage in others, until the market corrects them; and in some areas the market does not work well. But the very idea

that plenty is attainable—that there might be a material abundance to be equitably distributed—is singularly founded upon the enormous wealth produced by such a system.[22]

This is a celebration at once of the abundance of capitalism and of its comparative lack of waste. For the most part, goods and services that people want are produced, and those that are not wanted are avoided.

Given the ability of the market economy fueled by market liberty to coordinate activity, avoid waste, create wealth, and guarantee political liberty, the proper roles of the state are few. It should issue and control the supply of money. It should promote free international trade in currencies and in goods and services of all kinds.[23] It should maintain order. Friedman explicitly compares the state with an umpire in a game:

> Just as a good game requires acceptance by the players both of the rules and of the umpire to interpret and enforce them, so the good society requires that its members agree on the general conditions that will govern relations among them, on some means of arbitrating different interpretations of these conditions, and on some device for enforcing compliance with generally accepted rules. . . . These then are the basic roles of government in a free society: to provide a means whereby we can modify the rules, to mediate differences among us on the meaning of the rules, and to enforce compliance with the rules on the part of those few who would otherwise not play the game.

The concept of *order* turns out to be fundamental to the justification of the state and the definition of its scope:

> The organization of economic activity through voluntary exchange presumes that we have provided, through government, for the maintenance of law and order to prevent coercion of one individual by another, the enforcement of contracts voluntarily entered into, the definition of the meaning of property rights, the interpretation and enforcement of such rights, and the provision of a monetary framework.[24]

In short, the government should provide a narrow set of background institutions in which the market can operate.

Additional responsibilities of government are justified in Friedman's scheme by looking to "market failures," an idea that plays an important role in modern economic analysis of the public sector. The basic idea behind the concept of a market failure is that normal operations of the market—the ability of individuals to trade with one another—are impaired for one reason or another and desirable transactions blocked. Market failures are of several sorts, and Friedman uses them to generate an account of what the public sector should be doing. In Friedman's view, the state is as diverse as it should be when three kinds of market failures—public goods, neigh-borhood effects (or "externalities"), and technical monopolies—have been corrected.

It is universally claimed by economists, including Friedman, that a class of goods exists whose allocation on the basis of price fails because no mar-ket for the good will arise or, if it does arise, because not enough of the good will be produced. Within economics, these goods are designated by the term *public goods*. A classic example is national defense. There is a widespread desire on the part of citizens to have a defense against a com-mon foreign adversary. Defense is thus a good, but there is no way for the market to set a price for it.

The basic contrast betweeen public and private goods is simple. For private goods, say a hot dog at the ball game, a price can easily be set, and we can decide easily whether to pay it. No one else shares the hot dog. But how much sense does it make for me to pay for a given amount of defense? The answer is likely to be not much. Perhaps my fellow citizens will provide it, even if I do not participate. And, if they do, I will get the benefits even though I have not paid. A nuclear shield that protects them protects me. Knowing this, as someone deciding where to spend his money, I would rationally choose not to pay since the outcome for me is the same in either case; I'd try to get a "free ride." However, a general problem arises because my fellow citizens have the same thought. They will not pay in the hope that I will. As a consequence, either no defense or an insufficient amount is produced. The general statement of this dilemma is called the *free-rider problem*. The usual solution is government-administered financing of pub-lic goods.

The basic idea behind the concept of public goods is thus simple, but the seeming simplicity masks the complex issue of the scope of the state. The way in which terms are defined makes a lot of difference.[25] Friedman's def-inition of *public goods* turns on the concept of indivisibility:

> It is precisely the existence of . . . indivisible matters—protection of the in-dividual and the nation from coercion are clearly the most basic—that pre-vents exclusive reliance on individual action through the market. If we are to use some of our resources for such indivisible items, we must employ political channels to reconcile differences.[26]

Friedman uses *indivisible* to refer to goods from which there is no feasible way of excluding people who have not paid. National parks are not public goods in Friedman's view because it is easy to exercise control over entrances and exits. City streets are public goods in this sense, while toll roads are not. One of the most striking things about this definition is that it generates a very short list of public goods.

A second kind of market failure arises because the transactions of individuals, firms, and governments have positive and negative effects on others not party to the transactions. Typically, these market failures are called *externalities* to indicate that their effects on others are not reflected in the prices involved in voluntary transactions. Pollution of a stream is a real negative effect, but the pollutor often does not pay for all the consequences of the pollution. Friedman calls such market failures *neighborhood effects*. Here "strictly voluntary exchange is impossible when actions of individuals have effects on other individuals for which it is not feasible to charge or recompense them."[27]

As with the concept of *public goods*, a great deal turns on the definition of *externalities* or *neighborhood effects*. A broad definition will justify a functionally diverse state, a narrow definition only a minimal state. Obviously, Friedman has a way of generating a narrow definition. He reminds us that government intervention *itself* has a neighborhood effect: "We shall always want to enter on the liability side of any proposed government intervention, its neighborhood effect in threatening freedom, and give this considerable weight."[28] The argument is that, the more the government tries to fix externalities, the more of them it generates. Thus, the number of neighborhood effects or externalities that justify government intervention will be small, and, correspondingly, so too should the state.

The third kind of market failure that might justify government action involves technical monopolies, monopolies that "arise because it is technically efficient to have a single producer or enterprise." A ready example of such an enterprise is the provision of telephone service. Two telephone companies would be very inefficient, using more wire and requiring more maintenance than one company. But because a monopoly is needed does not prove that it should be a public monopoly. On the contrary, "The conditions making for technical monopoly frequently change and I suspect that both public regulation and public monopoly are likely to be less responsive to such changes in conditions, to be less readily capable of elimination, than private monopoly." Thus, Friedman's conception inclines greatly toward private unregulated monopoly, rather than public regulation of monopoly. But this is not to be taken as a hard-and-fast rule. Where the service or entity in question is essential and the power of the monopolist great, public "regulation or ownership may be a lesser evil."[29] Presumably, these examples will be few indeed.

It is often thought that one of the most obvious justifications of state action is the need to correct for inequalities of income, opportunity, etc. This line of reasoning has led to the creation of vast bureaucracies dealing with housing, health, and income transfers at the national and local levels. Are these activities justified?

For those cases in which such assistance is deemed to be justified, Friedman developed his proposal for the negative income tax. The basic idea of the negative income tax is to transfer money by means of the tax system, avoiding the necessity for complex bureaucracies administering diverse programs subject to various entitlement criteria. Instead of paying taxes, poor people who qualify are simply sent money by the government.

But how redistribution is accomplished is, of course, an entirely different question from whether it should be attempted at all. For Friedman, the question of whether the government has an obligation to alleviate poverty reduces to the question of whether poverty is a neighborhood effect or a public good:

> It can be argued that private charity is insufficient because the benefits from it accrue to people other than those who make the gifts—again a neighborhood effect. I am distressed by the sight of poverty; I am benefited by its alleviation; but I am benefited equally whether I or someone else pays for its alleviation; the benefits of other people's charity therefore partly accrue to me. . . . We might all be willing to contribute to the relief of poverty, *provided* everyone else did.
> . . . I [accept] . . . this line of reasoning as justifying governmental action to alleviate poverty; to set, as it were, a floor under the standard of life of every person in the community.[30]

There are at least two noteworthy features to this argument. First, it is framed in terms of tastes, not in terms of obligations. We should alleviate poverty if it offends us, but no argument as to why it should distress us is offered. Second, remember that governmental action to alleviate poverty has a presumption against it. If it is construed as a neighborhood effect, as the passage quoted above suggests, we have to remember that government action to alleviate the effect is *itself* a negative neighborhood effect because it will interfere with individual liberty, most notably the liberty of individuals to dispose of their income as they wish.

THE INEVITABILITY OF THE MARKET

Before moving on to a critical examination of these ideas, I want to add another historical observation. Besides the arguments of Friedman and other theoreticians of the Right, there is a deeper reality that brings the doctrines of the Right to the forefront of political conciousness. This is the phenomenon of the market itself, and it is felt in two all-permeating ways. First, the market dominates our experience. We spend the bulk of our lives working for money. We then spend the money on the goods made possible by a modern consumer society. Everything (and often everyone) appears to have its price. Transactions consume our time and our consciousness. Making money is what we do.

Second, taken on its own terms, the free self-regulating market—to the degree that it exists—is a great success. As virtually everyone now recognizes, capitalist countries simply do better than socialist or Communist countries at producing the goods and services that people want. Two hundred years ago, the bulk of the human population was poor; now, through the miracles of capitalism, hundreds of millions enjoy historically unparalleled affluence.

We are so accustomed to the hubbub of the market that it is easy to forget that a society organized around it is a recent—that is, approximately four-hundred-year-old—development. It is a form of social organization that displaced another. Dating the beginning of this trend in any given year is obviously arbitrary, but, during the period from 1500 to 1550, a transformation began in Europe that changed the ideas and material circumstances of our ancestors profoundly. The currents of commerce that ebbed and flowed in that period have become a flood tide today, a flood that seemingly sweeps all before it.

This transformation is still unfolding and, in the unfolding, creates a set of background conditions that make the philosophical doctrines of the Right seem, at one level at least, natural. To be against such ideas may seem to be against the trend of history, to oppose modernity itself.

Of course, human beings have traded things for as long as we have existed. In primitive societies, specialization arose, and the good spear maker might trade the weapon for the meat secured by the good spear thrower. But, until around 1500, transactions were subservient to, and drew their meaning from, the over-arching social systems in which people lived. Widespread equilibrium between supply and demand regulated by prices was the exception rather than the rule. Trade was carried on beyond local regions, but the bulk of commodities was produced and consumed locally, and it was the local social system that structured life. The movement away from this norm was slow and gradual until the Industrial Revolution of the eighteenth century, when it was greatly accelerated.

Prior to the Industrial Revolution, as Karl Polanyi puts it, "the economic system was submerged in general social relations; markets were merely an accessory feature of an institutional setting controlled and regulated by . . . social authority."[31] Of course, a great number of factors were involved in the movement toward the self-regulating market. The geographic isolation of the feudal town progressively broke down. Ocean charts and the other tools of navigation improved. The printing press facilitated the keeping of records and the dissemination of ideas. The wheels of commerce began to turn more quickly. Roads were built so that farmers could bring their produce to town in order to sell it.

By the time the Industrial Revolution really became established in the nineteenth century, the relation between the market and society had been turned on its head: markets now provided the framework for society, not the other way around. Polanyi notes that this transformation

> means no less than the running of society as an adjunct to the market. Instead of economy being embedded in social relations, social relations are embedded in the economic system. . . . Once the economic system is organized in separate institutions, based on specific motives and conferring a special status, society must be shaped in such a manner as to allow that system to function according to its own laws. This is the meaning of the familiar assertion that a market economy can function only in a market society.[32]

This replacement of one hierarchical order by a new one of course took hundreds of years in Europe. It required the redefinition of three elements of the old social order. Land, money, and labor had to be converted into commodities. That is, the status of the things in the old social order had to be denied and a new commercial status put in its place. A market in real estate had to be developed—until the 1600s in England, land was transferred primarily through inheritance. As a consequence, it did not end up in the hands of those who could earn the highest rate of return from it. National, or at least regional, labor markets had to be developed so that the availability of commodities would not be impeded by inadequate numbers of people to produce them. Medieval prohibitions against credit had to give way to make the formation of capital worthwhile.

But in America, where society had in effect broken with its feudal antecedents—that is, where there was no firmly entrenched, preestablished social order of perceived legitimacy—the emerging centrality of the market took hold more easily. Of course, the Americas did have a preexisting order—that of the Native Americans. But the European invaders did not accept the legitimacy of that order, and it was cast aside, with few qualms, by the mentality of commerce and the motive of gain.[33]

But, even in early nineteenth-century America, an agrarian social order existed, hindering the development of a market economy. That order was one of dispersed settlements—small towns and farms—that were largely self-sufficient. People grew their own food and built their own homes and barns with materials—lumber and stone—collected from their property. There simply were not many things to be bought, and the money income of most families was surely negligible. The market remained an ancillary enterprise.

The transformation of American society from agrarian to market oriented began in earnest after the Civil War and continues today. The trends are familiar. Industrialization and the need for large numbers of workers who work for a money wage, the attendant mechanization of agriculture and the resulting exodus from the farms—both contributed to urbanization. Once the population was overwhelmingly urbanized, the centrality of the market was cemented. In a city, you cannot be self-sufficient. To obtain the commodities necessary for life, you must have money. A properly functioning market becomes necessary for survival. The Great Depression was *great* because it took place in a world where, for the first time in human history, someone in the household had to have a *paying* job.

But these trends were even further intensified after World War II with first the promise and then the reality of mass affluence. Unprecedented numbers of people—millions upon millions—had more disposable income than they required for subsistence. Large-scale markets for luxuries developed. Through the magic of Madison Avenue, transmitted by television to a mass audience, wants were transformed into needs. In times of peace, the central task of the government became the management of the economy to create even more wealth for more people.

But, by the late 1970s, it looked like the great wealth machine was stalling. A growing chorus argued that, by overregulating the market, we were killing the goose that laid the golden egg.[34] We were interfering with the market. Devotees of the free market—partly on, partly off the political stage—reminded us over and over again that we had overstepped. We were impeding the (new) natural order. And, if the wages of sin were not death, they were almost as serious—the stagnation of the gross national product. In trying to fix our problems, however, we relied on a theory of the state that worsened rather than improved our condition, setting the stage for loss of trust in government.

Chapter 3

WHAT'S WRONG WITH THE RIGHT

The combination of economic and political *freedom* produced a golden age in both Great Britain and the United States in the nineteenth century.

MILTON AND ROSE FRIEDMAN, *Free to Choose*

The views of the Right that I have summarized are misguided on many levels and on many important points. I will save my most general criticisms of attempts to derive a theory of government legitimacy from market failures—an approach shared by liberal and conservative economists—for the next chapter. First, I want to point to large weaknesses in the Right's understanding of our choices, our language, ourselves and our morality, property rights, the relation between the market and the government, and history to prepare the way.[1]

MISREPRESENTING OUR CHOICES

Much of the rhetorical force of the argument of libertarian conservatives comes from the claim that the market is free and that the free market is a real alternative to coercion: "Economic freedom is an essential requisite for political freedom. By enabling people to cooperate with one another without coercion or central direction, it reduces the area over which political power is exercised. . . . The free market provides an offset to whatever concentration of political power may arise."[2] But the claim that the "free" market is a genuine alternative to coercion is false. The "free" market is necessarily coercive in a number of ways and simply could not function without force and the threat of force. No matter what economic model we rely on, the real choice that we have is not a simplistic alternative between

29

freedom and coercion but the more complicated choice of which forms of coercion to accept. Rather than illuminating this central moral and political question, the philosophy of the Right obscures, and even denies, its existence.

Friedman insists that "any form of coercion is inappropriate."[3] Astonishingly, *coercion* is never defined in *Capitalism and Freedom* or in *Free to Choose*, but the word is often invoked:

> No external force, no coercion, no violation of freedom is necessary to produce cooperation among individuals all of whom can benefit.

> The economic principles of Adam Smith . . . explain how it is that a complex . . . system can . . . flourish without central direction, how coordination can be achieved without coercion.

> Two parties who want to communicate . . . benefit from . . . agreement about the words they use. . . . At no point is there any coercion.

> Police forces are required to prevent coercion from . . . within. A major problem . . . is to assure that coercive powers granted to government to preserve freedom are limited to that function.[4]

Coercion seems to mean the use of force or the threat of force to compel someone to act or omit an action against his or her will.

It should be readily apparent that the "free" market goes hand and glove with coercion in this sense. The "free" market requires the prohibition of *completely voluntary* agreements between persons to fix prices, for instance, and such prohibition is effective only when coercion is available to enforce it. People who own firms tend to form monopolies to be able to control profits and increase prices. Friedman himself explicitly endorses deterring the formation of monopolies or breaking them up: "In practice, monopoly frequently, if not generally, arises from government support or from collusive agreements among individuals. . . . The problem is either to avoid governmental fostering of monopoly or to stimulate the effective enforcement of rules such as those embodied in our anti-trust laws."[5] Government intervention, backed by the threat of force, to prohibit, or reverse, such voluntary choices of the owners of the means of production is coercion. Collusion among *several* firms to fix prices is also prohibited by coercive means. To keep a "free" market open, the state therefore must coercively intervene to restrict the exercise of liberty.

Moreover, for the "free" market to work, it is also necessary that the government control externalities. Again, Friedman explicitly endorses coercion in certain cases, for example, those in which the activity of one person negatively affects another. The air pollution from a steel mill that dirties the Joneses' wash means that the mill is not paying the full cost of production. If the government steps in through regulation or tax to reduce pollution, it is coercing the owners of the mill to prevent them from shifting the cost to the Joneses. In fact, *any* regulation, tax, or court order designed to protect one person from being harmed by another or to shift the true cost of production to the producer requires the threat of force.

The "free" market also requires coercion when two parties have entered into an agreement—for something as basic and simple as a contract. Friedman calls for "the enforcement of contracts voluntarily entered into."[6] The market could not function without contracts, yet their enforcement requires force or the threat thereof. Through the civil courts, states can compel compliance with contracts. Maintaining the "free" market requires a military to repel or deter foreign invaders and police to protect citizens from one another. Securing tax dollars to support these activities requires coercion.

The assumption that the "free" market is not unavoidably tied to coercion is a crucial flaw in the conceptual framework of the Right. Their emphasis on voluntary individual actions leaves its proponents nothing to say when choices conflict. With respect to labor unions, Friedman writes, "Perhaps the most difficult specific problem in this area arises with respect to combinations among laborers, where the problem of freedom to combine and freedom to compete is particularly acute."[7] The Right has no hierarchy of liberties and no rules to adjudicate conflicts between liberties (or between liberty and any other value for that matter). But the state can and must make choices between different liberties all the time.

Nor did the "free" market somehow evolve without coercion. As was noted in chapter 2, what we call the "free" market developed in Europe over several hundred years as the feudal world collapsed. Far from supporting the notion that the "free" market is somehow natural, Polanyi's analysis shows that the establishment of the market was itself the result of intentional intervention: "Deliberate action of the state in the fifteenth and sixteenth centuries foisted the mercantile system on the fiercely protectionist towns and principalities."[8] Friedman seeks to redirect our visceral reaction against coercion toward the actions of the state he disapproves of, without acknowledging the demand for coercive actions that he himself calls for. In conservative rhetoric, *coercion* is a charge leveled at actions of the state that conservatives do not like.

This is an example of the way in which much of the intense loyalty to the doctrines of the Right flows from the misleading way in which alternatives are presented. It is not the only one. Friedman argues explicitly, for instance, that rejecting his doctrines puts us on the slippery slope toward socialism and tyranny: "There are only two ways of coordinating the economic activities of millions. . . . One is . . . the use of coercion—the technique of the army, . . . the other . . . the technique of the market place."[9] This is, of course, nonsense. Not one of the numerous industrialized democracies in Europe or the United States, Canada, Japan, New Zealand, Australia, etc., has a government organized along the lines advocated by Friedman. Are all these nations rushing down the road to dictatorship and the secret police? Is any of them?

The simple truth is that there are many forms of capitalism, with different mixes of regulation, social insurance, and redistribution. There is not one shred of empirical evidence to suggest that deviation from the extreme market orientation of the Right will lead to tyranny. The decision not to sell the Constitution to the highest bidder is not the first step on a well-greased slope to the Gulag. Most industrialized democracies appeal to an amalgam of ideas to justify government policy. Redistributive liberalism secures liberty of conscience and expression while guaranteeing that enough redistribution occurs to satisfy a standard of justice that is designed to mitigate the influence of things that are arbitrary from a moral point of view, for example, social and genetic accidents.[10] Another conception that finds expression in "the general welfare clause" of the Constitution holds that the state has the obligation to enhance the well-being of its citizens. Another conception might be called *civic democracy*, where the touchstone of legitimacy is the degree to which government policies reflect citizens' values. None of these ideas about what the state ought to be rules out a priori either democracy or capitalism.

Friedman misstates the nature of regulation. Not only may regulations be adopted by democratic processes, but due process is also available, making enforcement fair and appropriate rather than arbitrary and excessive. Under our laws, warning is typically required, there are procedures for hearings, the nature and timing of compliance can be negotiated, etc. The typical regulator can be readily and categorically distinguished from the Gestapo in the night. There is a tragic confusion here. Government interventions create liberties as well as limiting them. Effective air pollution regulations enhance the liberty of citizens to breathe clean air while at the same time restricting the liberty to drive or to use certain fuels. The presumption against government regulation is founded on a false presentation of alternatives.

Yet another false choice is set out in Friedman's defense of the unfettered market as the enemy of discrimination:

> It is a striking historical fact that the development of capitalism has been accompanied by a major reduction in the extent to which particular religious, racial, or social groups have operated under special handicaps in respect to their economic activities; have, as the saying goes, been discriminated against. . . . The preserves of discrimination in any society are the areas that are most monopolistic in character, whereas discrimination against groups of particular color or religion is least in those areas where there is the greatest freedom of competition.

The argument is that there are incentives built into capitalism that will tend to minimize discrimination: "The man who objects to buying from a Negro . . . thereby limits his range of choice. He will have to pay a higher price for what he buys."[11]

But suppose that discrimination exists in spite of market incentives against it? Friedman regards the issue as a matter of taste: "Is there any difference in principle between the taste that leads a householder to prefer an attractive servant to an ugly one and the taste that leads another to prefer . . . a white to a Negro, except that we . . . agree with one taste and may not with the other?"

Not that all tastes are the same:

> I deplore what seems to me the prejudice and narrowness of outlook of those whose tastes differ from mine in this respect and I think less of them for it. But in a society based on free discussion, the appropriate recourse is for me to seek to persuade them that their tastes are bad and that they should change their views and their behavior, not to use coercive power to enforce my tastes and my attitudes on others.[12]

No matter how flagrant and abusive—even life-threatening—the discrimination, it would on Friedman's view be wrong to use the powers of the state to protect those at risk. Here again we can easily see that the choice is *not* between coercion and liberty as Friedman would have us believe. Laws that force hospitals to admit poor blacks may threaten administrators with the coercive powers of the state. But poor blacks turned away from hospitals are also coerced, and in many cases the coercion costs them their lives. The real choice is on whose behalf the coercive powers of the state will be invoked. If you believe Friedman, those who suffer from discrimination in a capitalist society should not seek legislative or judicial relief. On the contrary, they should be grateful that they do not live in a dictatorship.

MISREPRESENTING LANGUAGE: THE COLLAPSE OF POLITICAL DISCOURSE

The treatment of discrimination in fact reveals even more serious difficulties. Friedman divides moral discourse into two large classes: the meaningful and the subjective. The meaningful set contains the words Friedman uses in *his* moral arguments: *liberty, coercion, public goods,* and *externalities.* Friedman insists that other moral argument occurs in the realm of tastes, in a vocabulary that forecloses meaningful discussion of what is at stake. Friedman's program is even more radical, and more fundamentally mistaken, than is normally understood. For him, all political discourse is meaningless unless it is carried on in his terms, those of money and markets. Congressional debates about policy are the theater of illusion, deliberations of the Supreme Court simply and only the subjective reports of the tastes of the Justices. Ordinary conversations between citizens concerning shared values and public purposes can *never* be understood as genuine and important argument.

The claim that other values represent merely tastes is not an accidental feature of Friedman's theory. Recognizing an alternative, broader vocabulary would automatically subject the free market to challenges from nonmarket considerations. We could constantly evaluate free market values against other values. Far better, from his point of view, to insist on a vocabulary in which no discussion can take place, in which by definition the market is supreme. But the confusion runs deeper still. Friedman's understanding of the place of tastes is fundamentally backward. The market, which now surges far beyond a level of consumption that can realistically be characterized as meeting real needs, *is* in the service of tastes. Yet, in Friedman's distorted worldview, it is real moral argument—which is indispensable to the functioning of democracy—that is labeled the expression of mere preference.

We can now see how precarious the coalition between the religious and the libertarian Right really is. If it stands for anything, the religious Right stands for the position that real moral claims exist and can be argued about. By nihilistically relegating all vocabulary other than his own to the realm of tastes, Friedman, however, implicitly dismisses the validity of *all* the arguments of the religious Right. An emphasis by liberals on the deep incompatibility of the libertarian and the religious Right might help undermine this coalition as a force in electoral politics.

MISREPRESENTING OURSELVES, OUR MOTIVES, AND OUR MORALS

Remember Friedman's central image: "Society consists of a number of independent households—a collection of Robinson Crusoes. . . . The household always has the alternative of producing directly for itself, it need not enter into any exchange unless it benefits from it. . . . Cooperation is thereby achieved without coercion."[13] In Robinson Crusoe, Friedman has invoked the wrong analogy for human existence.

Who was Robinson Crusoe? As Defoe describes him, he is an educated, headstrong, footloose, highly inventive, mercantile Englishman in the prime of his manhood who, on a voyage from South America to Africa, suddenly finds himself shipwrecked and—until the arrival of Friday— alone on an uninhabited island. *Robinson Crusoe* tells the story of how, with the abundant natural resources available to him on the island, and aided by stores and equipment salvaged from the wreck, Crusoe survives and even thrives. Compelling as this image of self-reliant man is, however, is it an appropriate one to apply to life in the real world?

Today, at the beginning of the last decade of the twentieth century, each square mile of earth is inhabited by an average of eighty-three people (thirty-two per square kilometer). In Europe and Asia there are over 233 people per square mile (ninety per square kilometer). Even in Polynesia there are eight people per square mile (three per square kilometer).

For the most part, people no longer live surrounded by the kind of natural environment that allows self-sufficiency. Forty percent of the world's population lives in urban centers. There are over 2,000 cities with more than 100,000 people. In thirty-six countries, a *majority* of the population lives in cities of over 500,000. Participation in markets could not possibly be voluntary for these people, or for 99 percent of the rest of us for that matter. In an urbanized market economy, few, if any, households have the alternative of producing directly for themselves. The claim that participation in the market is voluntary is patently false.

Crusoe, already a grown man and living alone, had only himself to support. In contrast, of the over 5 billion people in the world, 40 percent are either younger than fifteen years old or older than sixty-five. Worldwide there are 1,460 economically inactive persons for every 1,000 active ones.

This means that each modern-day Crusoe has to support another person and a half. Even in the United States, only 10 percent of the country's 250 million people live alone. There are over 64 million U.S. families. Of these, some 10.5 million are headed by single women. In addition to being fictional, Crusoe's life-style was highly abnormal—by today's standards at least.

Crusoe (luckily) was healthy and needed little health care. Unfortunately, the same cannot be said for the large numbers of poor and hungry around the world. Today, even as medicine is making almost unimaginable advances, increasing numbers of people have little or no access to medical care. Worldwide there is one physician for every 1,240 people, one nurse for every 540 people, one hospital bed for every 290 people, and one dentist for every 100,000 people. Public health spending averages $85.00 per person annually, ranging from $320 per person in the developed world to only $11.00 in the developing world. Infant mortality, a common measure of the quality of health care, follows this spending pattern: there are twenty infant deaths per thousand births in developed countries but at least 109 deaths per thousand in the developing countries. The worldwide average is ninety-seven deaths per thousand births.

Crusoe ate lavishly from the bounty of sea and land. Today the majority of the world's population consumes only 2,340 calories a day, 90 percent of the recommended minimum daily requirement for an adult. Crusoe's superior education saved him from peril several times and aided his efforts to make a comfortable home on his island. In the real world, only 67 percent of men and 54 percent of women can even read, and only 55 percent of men and 46 percent of women have received an education beyond grade school. Worldwide annual public education expenditures are $100 per person, and total education spending amounts to only $124. Even in the developed countries, annual spending on education, both public and private, amounts to only $435 per person.[14]

Our lives are not enchanting fictions. At any given time, hundreds of millions of people in the world are not in the prime of life but fragile and vulnerable. Even in "advanced" countries like the United States, many people in their prime cannot read and write or add and subtract. Many are passive, confused—incapable of conceiving, let alone executing, the ingenious solutions that make Robinson Crusoe so successful and attractive.[15]

Friedman's fundamental mistake is supposing that we can escape involuntary dependence on others, making a fantasy of independence into a conceptual building block for organizing our thinking about our obligations and society. The Crusoe analogy distorts the way we think about our obligations to others because it makes it appear that all obligations are matters of choice. In reality, we are not a collection of Robinson Crusoes acting independently, and not all obligations are voluntary. To think otherwise is absurd and misleading. Yet this position is crucial to the Right's view of the way in which society should be organized.

Closely connected with this misleading way of thinking about who we are is a misunderstanding of what motivates us. All actions, in one way or another, flow, Friedman says, from self-interest. In *Free to Choose*, Friedman writes, "Economic activity is by no means the only area of human life in which a complex and sophisticated structure arises as an unintended consequence of a large number of individuals cooperating while each pursues his own interests." But he is quick to point out that "self-interest is not myopic selfishness. It is whatever interests the participants, whatever they value, whatever goals they pursue."[16]

Taken narrowly, self-interest obviously offers too limited an interpretation of what we actually do. People do not, for example, simply try to maximize their incomes or even their own happiness. Much of human behavior is determined by explicit moral and religious values.[17] Noting these moral and religious motivations, economists often make the same move that Friedman does, interpreting the concept of self-interest so broadly that, in the end, it includes any behavior whatsoever. For instance, the firefighter who rushes into a burning building to save a child is, on this broader interpretation, acting in his own interest. The economist explains the action by appealing to the gratification that success would bring and the guilt of inaction, even if these were not conscious motives. Thus, the self-interest postulate is apparently saved. But, if self-interest is compatible with any state of affairs whatsoever, the proposition in question becomes impossible to test: any action whatsoever can be redescribed in terms of self-interest. *Self-interest* becomes a meaningless concept.

As no less than Darwin notes in *The Descent of Man*, "The first foundation or origin of the moral sense lies in the social instincts, including sympathy; and these instincts no doubt were primarily gained, as in the case of the lower animals, through natural selection."[18] Our motivations are concerned not just with our own survival and well-being but *necessarily* with the survival and well-being of our offspring—with our genes. Given the long periods of dependence in the human life cycle, people would simply not survive if a great deal of our behavior was not altruistic.[19] This instinctual behavior is strong within the family and, through education and positive and negative reinforcement, can be broadened to include a wider community. As the classical utilitarians like Mill and Edgeworth (from whose ideas Friedman's views are descended) noted, the issue is not whether there is altruistic behavior but, rather, which altruism to encourage. Friedman's mentor, Adam Smith, of course saw this and understood the importance of human sympathy in holding society together. In *The Theory of Moral Sentiments*, which Smith probably judged his most important work, he wrote, "How selfish soever man may be supposed, there are evidently some principles in his nature, which interest him in the fortune of others, and render their happiness necessary to him, even though he derives nothing from it, except the pleasure of seeing it."[20] But we do not get the whole of Smith's thinking in Friedman, just selected passages from *The Wealth of Nations*, where we start being deeply misled.

This misunderstanding of motivation is closely linked to mistakes concerning obligation. One of the fundamental messages of the Right is that one has no obligations except those chosen voluntarily, that only promises generate obligations. There is a sense, of course, in which our values are objects of choice. We can choose to accept or deny specific moral claims or moral theories or frameworks like Christianity or utilitarianism. We can also choose to accept or deny the theories of evolution and of relativity. But our obligations, like scientifically inferred mechanisms in the world such as natural selection, can exist independently of our assent to them. The notion of voluntaristic obligation is empty because it sheds no light on the question, For which obligations should I volunteer? We need some other consideration to which to appeal in deciding what to do. I agree to what I want, but what should I want?

One way to see how the voluntaristic model is misleading is to look at what we actually do. People everywhere recognize many obligations toward others that are not assumed voluntarily. Obligations not to harm others, for instance, are not the result of promises, and even the Right recognizes that these obligations exist. Indeed, the obligation not to harm others is a foundational principle for them. What obligations do we have toward our parents on the voluntaristic account? The obvious answer is none. We did not ask for the parents we got, and, of course, we did not ask to be born at all. Our consent has played no role. Therefore, if obligations can arise only through consent, no obligations need exist toward our parents. But, of course, everyone—or almost everyone—thinks that we do have obligations toward our parents, independent of promises, unless there has been severe abuse or the like. Those who abandon their parents financially, who cut off communication, who fail to provide vital assistance when needed, are outside the moral community.[21]

The problem of what obligations attach to roles assumed involuntarily is a generic one for the voluntaristic model on which the philosophy of the Right rests. As Robert Goodin puts it,

> Where roles have not been voluntarily assumed, and role responsibilities cannot therefore have been voluntarily incurred, advocates of the self-assumed-obligation model are left with an unenviable choice: either they must exempt every man, woman, and child who happens to occupy a role involuntarily from ordinary responsibilities attaching to that role; or they must concede that there are some special responsibilities that are not self-assumed. Surely the latter conclusion is more reasonable.[22]

For example, a person in a family who becomes the primary breadwinner through the death of a spouse has certain definite responsibilities even though the role was not assumed voluntarily.

We also believe that we have strong obligations toward our friends, but these are also difficult to fit into the voluntary contract model of obligation. We do not agree to be friends with someone in exchange for concern with our well-being. Rather, friendship grows out of shared experiences, problems, and yearnings. One of the characteristics of deep and lasting friendship is precisely that we do *not* know what we are bargaining for. Friendship is not a relationship with neat boundaries and inventories but an open-ended commitment to share the companionship and meet the needs of another person. A friend who breaks a promise or tells a lie violates another's trust, but the fundamental wrong is not the lying; rather, it is the taking advantage, the creation and exploitation of a vulnerability. The broken promise is a secondary offense.

The implausible individualistic premises revealed by the Robinson Crusoe analogy, combined with the mistaken reliance on the voluntaristic model of moral obligation, ironically lead to a misunderstanding of two paradigmatic conservative values: liberty and patriotism. No one enjoys the kind of liberty that Robinson Crusoe knew. Even those in the prime of life and wealthy depend on others for food, employment, safety, love and sex, self-respect, and so on, ad infinitum. No one who lives in any real human society, or in a real human family, much less a complex network of large public and private bureaucracies, is free from involuntary dependence on the will of others. I am unavoidably dependent on others I do not even know. Indeed, the market system makes us *more* dependent on unseen and unknown others than the more self-reliant world it replaced.

The Right also fails to see that its own account of liberty can yield reasons for redistributing resources. As we saw in chapter 2, Friedman offers no reasons for redistribution other than that he finds poverty distressing, which, of course, is not a reason. But our ability to make choices and act on them is heavily influenced and in many cases determined by our control over material resources. Without an education, I cannot be literate; without literacy, I cannot meaningfully participate in the political process. I may be free of legal restrictions on my conduct, and others may leave me alone, but I may still be unable to use my freedom. I may be free, but my liberty will be of little value.

The minimalist Right answers that the government should do no more than prevent and/or punish coercion of one person by another, set up rules of property, and establish procedures for the enforcement of contracts. But the enforcement of contracts requires a court system. A court system requires lawyers. And lawyers require money. The Right can hardly expect loyalty from those who are denied access to the central institutions by which the state protects the very rights that are its raison d'être. Redistribution of the resources necessary to make use of the legal system is required by the Right's own logic.[25]

What about access to the political process itself? Can we expect allegiance from people who are denied a voice in how the rules governing property are set simply because they do not have or cannot raise the money to run for public office? What this country needs is a mechanism ensuring adequate campaign financing for those interested in participating in the electoral process, and that will mean taking money from some for the benefit of others. And, of course, effective participation in the political process also requires literacy and nondiscriminatory registration. Are we not getting close to the welfare state that the Right set out to slay?

Conservatives might reply that the rights that they are defending are negative rights: all they require is that I not coerce you or deceive you in contracts. The rights they advocate are free, while those of the welfare state are expensive; the positive rights associated with the welfare state require violation of property rights, whereas the negative rights of the Right do not. But the distinction between positive and negative rights will not hold up.[26] Both positive and negative rights can cost money, and public money at that. The courts do not just cost the litigants; they cost the state money as well, money that must be raised by taxes. So do jails, and parole officers, and state and local police, and the Federal Bureau of Investigation, and the Drug Enforcement Administration.

The secular Right cannot make sense out of patriotism either. Political actors on the Right appeal to patriotism, while at the same time their theorists deny the possibility of being patriotic. On the very first page of *Capitalism and Freedom*, Friedman chides President Kennedy for his inaugural query, "Ask not what your country can do for you—ask what you can do for your country." According to Friedman, "To the free man, the country is a collection of individuals who compose it. . . . He regards government as a means, an instrumentality."[27] But patriotism depends at least in part on an identification between the self and the nation—which of course includes the government. Try rewriting the Gettysburg Address while thinking of government along the lines advocated by Friedman: "Four score and seven years ago our fathers brought forth on this continent, an insurance company. . . ." Robinson Crusoe felt little tie to place or nation-state, but that is true of few of us. A culturally conservative commitment to patriotism is inconsistent with the libertarian economist's vision of government. But the demise of patriotism is only the tip of the iceberg. In the worldview of the Right, the government can in no way appropriately express and reflect who we are or who we aspire to be.

MISREPRESENTING GOVERNMENT

In a section entitled "Government as Rule Maker and Umpire," Friedman writes, "These then are the basic roles of government in a free society: to provide a means whereby we can modify the rules, to mediate differences among us on the meaning of the rules, and to enforce compliance with the rules on the part of those few who would otherwise not play the game." He claims that "the organization of economic activity through voluntary exchange presumes that we have provided, through government, . . . the definition of the meaning of property rights."[28] He is saying that his conception of government rests on a theory of property rights, but he never defends or even defines those rights. Friedman's discussion of property rights in *Free to Choose*, for instance, is limited to two pages.[29] One of these pages praises the high percentage of home ownership in America and complains about the high rate of corporate income tax. The other is a rambling, and in my judgment disingenuous, discussion of the unfairness of inheritance taxes.[30] In *The Essence of Friedman*, a book of over five hundred pages,

drawing together Friedman's work over several decades, property rights—
if one can believe the index—are discussed only twice, and both times in
the context of discussions of the defects of the Yugoslav property system![31]
According to Friedman, one of the few legitimate functions of government
is to define property rights. He writes volumes, but never gets to this subject. But, once the problem is set up as Friedman would have it, without a
theory of property rights we cannot tell what it is that government is supposed to do. If, for example, there are property rights to medical care, the
role of government changes drastically.

Absent clarity about property rights, we are left with the claim that government is umpire. The ideal umpire in the National League never interferes with a baseball game unless someone breaks the rules, or a leg. If he
happens to dodge the wrong way and inadvertently interferes with a play,
this is regarded as an error. If it happens too often, he will be dismissed.
Friedman believes that the government's role in the national life is similar,
but the comparison is misleading at best. The differences between governing a nation and umpiring a baseball game are numerous. Life is not a game.
The rewards and punishments of life are of a different order than those
awarded or suffered on the playing field. In a game, the rules are unani-
mously accepted by the players. No governmental rule enjoys unanimous
assent.

MISUNDERSTANDING THE RELATION OF
ECONOMICS TO GOVERNMENT

It may appear that Friedman has a line of argument open to him that would
be immune to the criticisms I have made. He contends that we should have
a state big enough, but only big enough, to correct market failures. His
claim is that economic theory itself, leaving aside political theory, provides
a justification of the minimum, but only the minimum, state.[32] I have more
to say about this general approach to government in chapter 4, but here I
show how Friedman's particular lack of an underlying moral framework
undercuts his ability to make this argument.

Recall that there are three kinds of market failures: public goods, technical monopolies, and externalities or neighborhood effects. But exactly
how do we specify these failures? At least two of the key terms, *public goods*
and *externalities*, prove to be formal terms only. The concepts themselves
cannot tell us which externalities to control and which public goods to
produce. Let us start with public goods.

Recall that Friedman understands public goods to be goods that have the characteristic of nonexcludability, goods for which there is no feasible way to limit their enjoyment only to those who are willing to pay for them. The state should step in to produce only nonexcludable goods. Again, by this definition, there are few public goods. Many parks and museums (which are excludable) would not exist under Friedman's scheme, for instance, since private markets would not produce them. I suspect that this radical result is at least a factor in the search of economists who are not devotees of the Right for alternative definitions of public goods.[33] "Nonrivalness" is often advanced as an alternative or supplemental definition. "Nonrival" public goods are those for which one person's consumption or use does not interfere with another's. Yellowstone National Park is not a public good under Friedman's definition, but, at least up to certain congestion levels, it passes the nonrivalness test. My presence in the park does not interfere with your presence in it; thus, on this definition, a park is a public good, a proper responsibility of government.

But the nonrivalness definition can lead us astray in the opposite direction; it can legitimize too much state action. Suppose that I plan to drive to New York City this afternoon by myself in a large sedan. Is the empty back seat a public good? It would seem so by the nonrivalness definition. Now, the only way to avoid the absurd implication that the back seat of my car is a public good is by invoking some conception of property rights or privacy. Therefore, to bound the concept of a public good properly, the state must define property rights, privacy, and related issues independently.

It is important to see that this problem is quite general. It is possible to define this form of market failure only after many questions about the scope of the state have been decided on other grounds.[34] In other words, some normative conception of the state necessarily lies behind—is logically prior to—what we take to be a public good. So the concept of a public good cannot itself be the foundation for deciding how big the state should be.

Similar problems plague the concept of externalities.[35] Pollution of a stream is typically taken as a negative externality. It is hard for all the people harmed by the pollution to coordinate their activities and collect damages from the polluter. So Friedman seems comfortable with at least some minimal environmental regulation. But it is very hard to tell where the boundary of the concept of externality lies. People affect one another's well-being in numerous positive and negative ways that are difficult for the market to capture: pollution of a stream, noise from an aircraft, junkyards, plunging necklines, Sinatra crooning from the jukebox, cleaning up junkyards, pink houses, burning crosses, a clear view of the Statue of Liberty, rock music blaring at the beach, rock music being turned off at the beach. The list could go on and on. If we try to regulate all these activities, we will have a functionally diverse state indeed. So we need some standard by which to decide what should be regulated and what not. The concept of externality itself cannot supply this limit; only an account of the proper role of government can. So the concept of externality is usable only after the issue of the scope of government has been settled on independent grounds.[36] And for those grounds we need to go beyond economic theory to political and moral concepts that Friedman does not supply, relegating them instead to matters of taste.

This is more than a logical puzzle. The failure of externalities to define their own limits leaves it open for Friedman to appeal vaguely to the negative neighborhood effect of government intervention and argue de facto for correcting very few externalities at all. Contrary to Friedman's claim that the free market makes everyone better off, an unregulated market can and often does make everyone worse off. With externalities uncontrolled, the self-interested behavior of individuals can lead to a world in which the well-being of everyone is impaired. Pollution caused by leaded gasoline, for instance—even if that gasoline made each person's car run better—could eventually make everyone worse off if not controlled. Failure to control externalities gives private action so much scope that it threatens the commons, recalling Oliver Goldsmith's poem:

> The law locks up the man or woman
> Who steals the goose from off the Common
> And leaves the greater villian loose
> Who steals the common from the goose.

Without a robust conception of externalities, it is Friedman who leaves the greater villian loose, the one who steals the common from the goose.[37]

Although Friedman's arguments do not work, it is of vital importance to see how their apparent success has undercut our well-being. Friedman has taken the framework of welfare economics, derived from economists like Marshall, Pigou, and Samuelson, and pulled it in the direction of a functionally sparse state by restricting the definition of public goods; by arguing that government intervention is itself an externality, thus limiting the degree to which the government may legitimately step in to internalize the costs of production; and by claiming that government itself is the primary source of monopoly, thus diverting attention from the role of economic concentration in the private sector. Public lands that are not nonexcludable have been declared excess. Under the guise of the "free" market, there has been a focus on cutting the "regulatory burden," with success defined in many cases by the number of pages of regulation that have been eliminated.[38] The savings-and-loan disaster is simply one example of cutting regulations with monumental adverse consequences for the public. Opportunities to capture the benefits of competition that, were it not for the arguments of the Right, would be a centerpiece of a government oriented to the "free" market have also been passed up.[39] As a consequence, there has been an enormous concentration of economic power in a variety of sectors of our economy.

MISREPRESENTING THE PAST

Although the compromises of politics have fortunately limited the extent to which the Right's ideas have become policy, it is important to see how radical the effects would be if those ideas were implemented. If our choice is between the free market or the army, we will choose the free market, even completely unregulated. If we have no obligations other than those arising from promises, there is likely to be little or no concern for the poor. If all vocabulary other than that of the market is in the domain of tastes, there is no moral or political ground to limit the market, and those with the most economic power will prevail.

The utopian notion that society can be properly organized through the "free" market is not a reflection of the natural human condition but rather the result of relatively recent historical accidents. Such schemes were tried in England and America in the nineteenth century and rejected because of their unacceptable consequences. But the effects of this failed experiment, which Friedman cites as a golden age, reverberate throughout the world today over 150 years later.

The gradual movement from feudal society to the world of the self-regulating market took centuries, but it is possible to date the beginning of a utopian market society in England authoritatively. By the early nineteenth century, markets for land and for money had been established. In 1834, the Speenhamland Laws, which were originally enacted in 1795 and which replaced other labor regulations and protected the poor against destitution, were suddenly abolished. As Polanyi summarizes it,

> Under Elizabethan Law the poor were forced to work at whatever wages they could get and only those who could obtain no work were entitled to relief;

relief in the *aid of wages* was neither intended nor given. Under the Speenhamland Law a man was relieved even if he was in employment, as long as his wages amounted to less than the family income granted to him by the scale. Hence, no laborer had any material interest in satisfying his employer, his income being the same whatever wages he earned. . . . Within a few years the productivity of labor began to sink to that of pauper labor, thus providing an added reason for employers not to raise wages. . . .

On the face of it the "right to live" should have stopped wage labor altogether. Standard wages should gradually have dropped to zero, thus putting the bill wholly on the parish, a procedure which would have made the absurdity of the arrangement manifest. But this was an essentially pre-capitalist age, when the common people were traditionally minded, and far from being directed in their behavior by monetary motives alone.[40]

Speenhamland was unstable, its productivity costs too great. These "right to live" guarantees were abolished in two stages in 1832 and in 1834 under the heading of Poor Law Reform:

> In 1834 industrial capitalism was ready to be started, and Poor Law Reform ushered in. The Speenhamland Law which had sheltered rural England, and thereby the laboring population in general, from the full force of the market mechanism was eating into the marrow of society. By the time of its repeal huge masses of the laboring population resembled more the specters that might haunt a nightmare than human beings. But if the workers were physically dehumanized, the owning classes were morally degraded. The traditional unity of a Christian society was giving place to the denial of responsibility on the part of the well-to-do for the conditions of their fellows. The Two Nations were taking shape. To the bewilderment of thinking minds, unheard-of wealth turned out to be inseparable from unheard-of poverty. . . .
>
> The mechanism of the market was asserting itself and clamouring for its completion: human labor had to be made a commodity. Reactionary paternalism had tried in vain to resist this necessity. Out of the horrors of Speenhamland men rushed blindly for the shelter of a utopian market economy.[41]

The stage was set for the utopian experiment in the self-regulating market.

The result was the emergence of unrestricted free market capitalism, which led to social catastrophe in nineteenth-century England. While the Industrial Revolution and laissez-faire economics brought fantastic wealth to the middle and upper classes, conditions for the poor and the working class were dreadful. This scandalous level of human suffering inspired the various socialist movements of the period, which would culminate in capitalism's foremost challenge, communism.

In 1845, Friedrich Engels published the landmark *The Condition of the Working-Class in England*, documenting the horrible conditions in the factories and the countryside. He was clear about the role that this suffering played in encouraging alternatives to laissez-faire capitalism:

> The condition of the working-class is the real basis and point of departure of all social movements of the present because it is the highest and most unconcealed pinnacle of the social misery existing in our day. French and German working-class Communism are its direct, Fourierism and English Socialism, as well as the Communism of the German educated bourgeoisie, are its indirect products. A knowledge of proletarian conditions is absolutely necessary to be able to provide solid ground for socialist theories, on the one hand, and for judgments about their right to exist, on the other; and to put an end to all sentimental dreams and fancies pro and con.[42]

The conditions that Engels wrote about were indeed inhuman. The slums were horrific.[43] Unbridled competition encouraged fraud and "adulteration" of goods, which afflicted the poor more than the rich, who could afford to buy higher-quality goods. There was a revolution in the structure of family life as women and children workers replaced men in the mills and factories.[44] The poor conditions and long hours generated heretofore unknown health problems.[45] In the rural areas, where most people had now become day laborers, the new regime brought great vulnerability: "One or two days without work in the course of a month must inevitably plunge such people into the direst want. Moreover, they cannot combine to raise wages, because they are scattered."[46] At the same time, the "Game Laws" made it illegal for laborers to hunt or catch wild game, preserving the privilege for the rich and landed few.[47]

Many proponents of the free-market and laissez-faire capitalism often forget this period of incredible human suffering. But they also forget that citizens and governments in that earlier time quickly recognized the dangers of unregulated markets and stepped in to constrain them. Regulations were issued restricting work hours per day, legalizing unions and strikes, improving sanitation in the slums, etc.[48] Although only partially successful in mitigating the misery of the working class, these efforts show how an earlier society realized that the "free" market was not what it wanted. Engels observed that many industrialists also endorsed regulations that they had formerly opposed, as they came to realize the value of government regulation in restricting competition.

Because of its brutal and essentially dangerous nature, utopian capitalism has been progressively restricted by the refeudalization of labor, land, and money: "Leaving the fate of soil and people to the market would be tantamount to annihilating them. Accordingly, the countermove consisted in checking the action of the market in respect to the factors of production, labor, and land. This was the main function of interventionism."[49] Polyani dates the height and then the sudden collapse of the utopian experiment in free markets to the beginning of the first great war in 1914, although its unraveling certainly began earlier. Much of the fabric of our society is built around the repudiation of that earlier failed experiment. With mechanisms from labor laws to the establishment of the central banks, all contemporary governments put firm limits on the operation of "free" markets.

Unfortunately, government control and regulation of the free market was not the only reaction to this market experiment. Another branch of the catastrophe engulfed Russia, Eastern Europe, and China when brutal and repressive Communist dictatorships were thought justified by Marxist doctrines proposed to protect the workers from the exploitation of capitalism. The environmental movement of the 1970s and the rise of the "green" parties in Europe are attempts to remove land, and nature in general, at least in part, from the workings of the market. They are attempts to build a new order, one based on a vision of humans as a part of nature, to circumscribe more fully still the workings of the free market.

Chapter 4

THE FAILURE
OF MARKET FAILURES

What is at issue now is the dominance of money outside its sphere.

MICHAEL WALZER, *Spheres of Justice*

Much of the credibility of Friedman's false and misleading ideas about the market and government depends on their apparent familiarity. They are derived from a far more widespread theory of state legitimacy embraced by the centrist and even liberal think tanks discussed in chapter 1: the general idea that the main role of the state is to correct for market failures. At one level, the Right simply adopts the mainstream vocabulary and gives it new and distorted meaning. Even without distortions, however, the mainstream conception fails to yield an adequate theory of state legitimacy. It is because of this failure—the failure of market failures—that an alternative account of the role of the state is necessary.

The mainstream market failure theory of governmental legitimacy is taught everywhere in undergraduate economics courses. It is often the central catechism in professional schools of public policy such as Harvard's John F. Kennedy School of Government, which was founded in the 1960s to educate people to serve in public office and spawned about twenty similar programs around the United States. As the graduates of these programs penetrate all levels of government, these mistaken ideas become more widespread.[1]

PERILOUS PEDIGREE

The primary difference between the centrist derivation of government responsibilities from market failures and that of the Right is that centrists rely on a moral theory to ground their understanding of proper state action, a

49

theory that informs what they mean by externalities, public goods, and the harm from monopolies. It is a moral theory that keeps the centrist use of market failures from sliding into disastrously laissez-faire public policy. In *A Primer for Policy Analysis*, Edith Stokey and Richard Zeckhauser of the Kennedy School state, "The purpose of public decisions is to promote the welfare of society." In reaching this objective, "Government participation in the resource allocation processes of society can be justified on two grounds only: 1. *Equity*: A more desirable distribution of goods and services among the members of the society is fostered. 2. *Efficiency*: Efficiency is promoted in situations where the market has failed."[2]

Efficiency is defined in terms of the number of people getting what they want through the marketplace, constrained only by their incomes. Efficiency is brought about by correcting for the same market failures that Friedman lists, but market failures understood differently. Public goods are defined as both nonexcludable and nonrival. There is no presumption against government trying to control externalities. And government is not seen as a primary source of monopoly. While the tradition in which the *Primer* is written contains many insights about how to improve human well-being that the Right discards, taken by itself it cannot—as these and numerous other authors suppose—generate an adequate theory of state legitimacy.

In seeking to maximize human welfare, the market failure framework has descended from and embraced utilitarianism. As formulated by John Stuart Mill, this doctrine "holds that actions are right in proportion as they tend to promote happiness, wrong as they tend to produce the reverse of happiness."[3] We should seek, according to utilitarians, the greatest happiness for the greatest number. In the philosophical literature written since the Second World War, there have been numerous serious criticisms of this doctrine. Market failure literature proceeds, however, as if this other literature did not exist.

Of the several important and often-cited problems with utilitarianism, three are most important from the point of view of public policy.[4] First, utilitarianism conflates collective choice with individual choice. On the utilitarian model of decision making, individuals act to maximize their own happiness. Each of us has a rough, although perhaps only implicit, set of priorities to which we appeal in deciding how to spend our various constrained resources (time, money, energy, etc.) to reach those objectives that will most increase our happiness. But, when we move to the level of social choice, insurmountable problems arise because persons, especially in a deeply pluralistic society such as that of the United States, have disparate, incommensurable ends.

Second, utilitarianism is in principle compatible with severe violations of human rights if total utility will be maximized by such violations. Jeremy Bentham, an early utilitarian, showed open contempt for the idea of human rights: "Natural rights is simple nonsense; natural and imprescriptible rights, rhetorical nonsense, nonsense on stilts."[5] Whether to reinstitute slavery will always be an open question to the utilitarian: slavery will be acceptable if it results in a net increase in total utility, unacceptable only if it does not.

Third, by its very nature, utilitarianism is indifferent with respect to the distribution of utility among parties as long as the greatest total utility is attained. Thus, utilitarianism has nothing principled to say to questions of public policy that concern the equitable distribution of benefits and burdens. Although Stokey and Zeckhauser cite reasons of equity as one of the bases for governmental intervention, they provide no discussion whatsoever about the concept.[6] Their implicit political philosophy of utilitarianism is noncommittal on questions of distribution.

Part of what lies behind the centrist allegiance to utilitarianism is a parochial conception of what rationality is. Instrumental definitions of rationality have two parts: an *end*, specified somehow, and *means* that are to be used in reaching the end. Rational behavior is taken to be that which uses the most efficient means to reach desired ends. Maximizing utility is one end, but there are numerous others, such as righteousness, doing what one's role requires, maximizing liberty, protecting the vulnerable, maximizing justice, etc. Writers like Stokey and Zeckhauser who hold that rational action will seek to maximize individual and social utility alone confuse *a* definition of rationality with *the* definition. Centrist political economists thus tend to end up dismissing important moral issues that cannot be discussed in terms of utility maximization—much as Friedman did—as mere tastes. These defects in moral theory point to a hole at the center of their larger theory of state legitimacy, one that calls out to be filled by a view that can accommodate a richer moral language.

DISCOUNTING

The market failure approach to state legitimacy also fails to supply a coherent way of thinking about the future.[7] As this framework is typically used, it assumes that third parties are only contemporary human individuals, fellow citizens now alive.[8] That this assumption is being increasingly questioned even within the market failure tradition in the literature dealing with long-term problems such as nuclear waste disposal suggests the need for a new framework. The conventional approach fails altogether to come to grips with long-term global threats like the greenhouse effect that are driven by our energy choices. The market failure approach normally involves an inappropriate use of discounting.

The conception of human nature implicit in the philosophies of both the center and the Right assumes that individuals seek to maximize their gains from exchange by acting in a "rational" (self-interested) way to achieve certain ends.[9] How does a person so conceived think about future events? She discounts for them. Money has a time value: "The present value of $1 payable next year is $1/(1 + r)$. This is the amount which, if invested today at an annual interest rate, r, will yield $1 in one year."[10] A person who thinks this way will typically pay less now for something that will not be received until sometime in the future than for the same thing in the present. (Discounting is done in terms of real rates of interest, thus ignoring inflation.)

The time value of money can be broken into different components: one is the opportunity costs of missed chances to invest. Waiting a year for the money means that I forgo the interest I could have earned on it through investment. Accordingly, I should discount what I will give today for a dollar a year from now by how much it has cost me to forgo the interest. Risk is another factor in the time value of money. There is some possibility that the person promising to give me a dollar a year from now will not. He or she may die, go broke, move away, forget the promise, etc. I should, insofar as it is possible, assign some degree of probability to these events and discount the present value of the dollar by some additional amount.

What is striking about this way of thinking about future investments is how steeply values decline even at relatively low rates of interest. The present value of a dollar twenty years from now at 5 percent interest is 37.7 cents; in forty years it is 14.2 cents. At ten percent in twenty years the dollar's present value is 14.9 cents, and a dollar paid in forty years is now worth 2.2 cents! For this reason, discount tables rarely go beyond forty years. On a discounted-dollar basis, the world that my six-year-old daughter will inhabit when she is about my age is barely worth thinking about. Forget altogether the world her children will inhabit.

The conventional conceptual tools of the Right and the center cannot supply a coherent way to think about long-term obligations. All systematic accounts of morality require what I would like to call *role reciprocity.* "Do unto others as you would have them do unto you" is a requirement of respect. Respecting others as free and reasonable persons should not depend on their proximity to us in time. We are led away from thinking respectfully about persons (and events) in the future by the concept of discounting, by framing our responsibility for that future in terms of our own returns on investment. Once we think about who we are and what we should do the way Friedman and Stokey and Zeckhauser urge us to, it is irrational not to assign a low value to benefits that accrue in the distant future. *Any* positive rate of discount at all will have the effect of assigning values of no practical consequence to future events beyond the next few years.

Discounting causes us to misunderstand our obligations toward the future, by conflating factors correlated with time, such as opportunity costs and risk, with time itself.[11] Its logic is just as misguided as if we thought that obligation decreased with distance. Consider our response to a famine in East Africa. We might think of ourselves as excused from responding as individuals because we have competing moral commitments and were not the cause of the situation, because providing for the citizens of other countries is the responsibility of their own governments, because our government should do it on our behalf, etc. What we will *not* offer as a moral reason is merely that the people in need are far away.

When we think about public policy in terms of markets and discounting, we fail to distinguish between two concepts: animal time and deep time. In a few families, five generations may sit around a festive table at Thanksgiving—almost never more. These five generations form the rough outer boundary of our sense of time as animals. A wider view of nature gives a sense of deep time. John McPhee wrote in *Basin and Range,* "A million years is a short time. . . . You begin tuning your mind to a time scale that is the planet's time scale. For me, it is almost unconscious now and is a kind of companionship with the earth."[12] The conceptual framework proposed by the Right and the center for thinking about public policy barely comprehends five generations of animal time and simply cannot deal with deep time. To the degree that we rely on this framework, we are led away from thinking about future events that will occur in deep time. Thus, potentially disastrous effects like climate change, the thinning of the earth's protective ozone layer, the loss of topsoil, the dispersion of heavy metals into the environment, and widespread deforestation are dismissed as inappropriate subjects of government attention.

There is, of course, nothing wrong with discounting as a tool for thinking about investments in replaceable things like computers and tractors. Discounting allows us to compare our choices as their effects play out over time. But the reasonable rule to follow in the use of this tool is that its value is inversely proportional to the replaceability of the asset in question. No one would think of discounting the Constitution—stored under glass in the National Archives—by allowing schoolchildren to take little snips of it. The biosphere itself is treasured and revered by most people and is certainly an irreplaceable asset.[13] (I return to the topic of the environment in detail in chapter 7.)

DUBIOUS THEOLOGY / HUMAN DOMINION

Works like those of Friedman and Stokey and Zeckhauser typically uncritically assume that it is appropriate to think of nonhuman life on earth, and even the earth itself, solely in terms of its use for humans. As is well known, there are some phrases in the Book of Genesis that seem to support this view.[14] Key features of this doctrine are that human beings are a separate order of creation from the earth itself and that the world was made by God for their use. It is an assessment of the human condition that emerged from the worldview of roughly 1000 B.C. As that worldview has been called into question, the attendant understanding of the status of human beings has eroded. Recently, many theologians have been emphasizing a different aspect of our biblical heritage, one based in part on different sections of Genesis.[15] Many Christians, as well as adherents of other religions, believe that the earth belongs to God and that the men and women living on it are merely stewards.

Ideas of stewardship also come from nonreligious sources, major scientific developments having undercut, if not necessarily overthrown, the belief in human dominion. Findings from geology demonstrate that the earth is billions of years old and has undergone numerous transformations. The theory of evolution shows that there has been a continuum of living things. Admittedly, rising affluence and urbanization in the industrialized countries—which have decreased our *immediate* dependence on agriculture and forests—have permitted, and then fostered, nonutilitarian attitudes toward nature.[16] However, as we see ourselves in the context of our origins and as part of a complex and interactive whole, the notion that we are supreme masters of nature becomes more and more implausible. As Aldo Leopold has noted in *A Sand County Almanac*, the more we see ourselves as the product of nature, the more we see ourselves as the stewards of it.[17]

A final very practical fact that makes it necessary to change our view of the relation between humans and the biosphere is the threat that the scale of human activity is becoming too large for the biosphere, on which it depends, to support.[18] When environmental problems are taken seriously at all in the market failure tradition, they are seen as issues of not having the price right, of needing to internalize the costs of production, or of controlling neighborhood effects. Whether the biosphere can support ever larger numbers of people consuming more and more is a question that is not even asked. While Robinson Crusoe lived alone on a large island, nearly 5.5 billion people now live together on our small planet. Surely it is time to rethink the grounds of our political and social philosophies.

WHY EVERYTHING IS NOT AND SHOULD NOT BE FOR SALE

Perhaps most important, neither the libertarian nor the mainstream conceptions of government legitimacy can make sense of the limits of the market. In their obsession, proponents of the market gloss over, or perhaps do not even recognize, that there are certain unavoidable questions that a market-oriented view is incapable of answering. Perhaps economists of the Right and the center have implicitly admitted this: while they have spent a great deal of time describing the financial requisites of the market, they have paid little or no attention to its moral foundations. However, questions of morality cannot be avoided when formulating public policy.

The Right and the center argue—or assume—that everything should be open for trading in the market, all else being equal, but their conceptual terms do not allow them to specify what *all else being equal* means. Friedman himself even proposes a constitutional amendment, one "patterned after the Second Amendment (which guarantees the right to keep and bear arms): *The right of the people to buy and sell legitimate goods and services at mutually acceptable terms shall not be infringed by Congress or any of the States.*"[19] But he offers no guidance on what he means by *legitimate* and hence cannot answer, or even intelligently discuss, the moral questions, What should be for sale? On what terms should *x* be for sale?

Let us begin by depicting markets and all goods and services separately (see fig. 1). A strict market-oriented approach to public policy offers no bounds on what should be traded on the market. Since the few responsi-

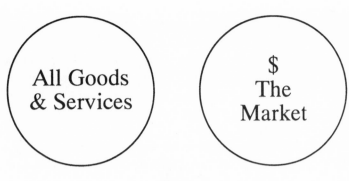

Figure 1

Figure 2

bilities of the state, like defense, are thought of as market failures, we need not represent them separately; once the state has acted, the market has been "corrected" and is thus in theory functioning properly. Merged, the ideal world simply looks like one circle (see fig. 2). This picture, however, is very misleading. We can begin to see how by again asking the question, What should be for sale? For the hard-liners of the Right, the answer is everything. Many in the center do not even entertain the question.

But many of the toughest questions in public policy involve deciding what should be for sale. The headlines are filled with these debates. Should sex be for sale? If so, all kinds of sex, or just some? And sold where? And how? What about drugs? If some drugs, which ones, and why? Abortions? Public land? If some public land, which land? Medications of questionable usefulness like laetrile? Rights to drill for oil in the Santa Barbara Channel? Should all domestic markets be open to fair foreign competition, or only some? How should *fair* be defined? Should the right to pollute be for sale?

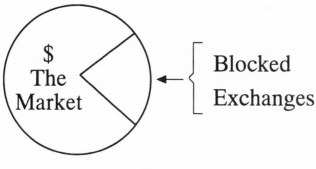

Figure 3

The right to hunt? Attendance at bullfights or cockfights? Adult pornography? Pornography involving the torture of animals? Prime farmland for a bowling alley? Civil War battlefields? "Saturday night" specials? Grenade launchers? Fully automatic weapons? Jet fighters? The *Constitution* (the ship)? The Constitution (the piece of paper)?

What is not now legally for sale? A partial list would include professorships in economics (the irony of this prohibition seems completely to escape some advocates of the market),[20] human beings, many forms of political influence, citizenship, criminal justice, First Amendment rights, the right to more than one spouse, exemption from the draft (when there is one), jury duty, sex, certain drugs, designated wilderness areas, certain awards (the Congressional Medal of Honor), human organs (eyes, kidneys, hearts), life-threatening items (flammable shirts and new cars without seatbelts), the right to shoot a bald eagle, the Statue of Liberty, a hired assailant. These are what Michael Walzer calls "blocked exchanges."[21] A black or grey market exists in many of these areas, but these transactions typically have neither legal nor, in most cases, social sanction. So the situation is now provisionally as depicted in figure 3. But the line between blocked and permitted exchanges is shifting and open to argument. Should babies be for sale? Human organs?[22] Should we allow concessions in national parks? Should we legalize prostitution? Many of the important issues of public policy are about what should be bought and sold.

The situation becomes even more complicated when it is recognized that there are two kinds of blocked exchange. One kind involves goods that are not legally available at all. Certain drugs and the pelts of some animals that are in danger of extinction are examples of things for which society seeks, for widely accepted reasons, to ensure a supply of zero. The second kind

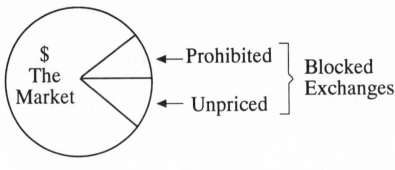

Figure 4

of blocked exchange involves another class of "goods" a supply of which continues to exist but that cannot be bought or sold (e.g., babies for adoption, organs for transplantation). Here society does not try to reduce the supply to zero but blocks any market-like transactions. Let us call these two kinds of blocked exchanges, respectively, *prohibited exchanges* and *unpriced exchanges*. In the light of these considerations, we should revise figure 3 as shown in figure 4.

By selecting a framework for analysis that assumes that markets should operate everywhere, the market disciples embrace a principle that is at once too strong and too shallow. It is too strong in that it assumes that all arguments in favor of blocked exchanges must fail. It is too shallow in that it provides no grounds for deciding—and not even any vocabulary for discussing—many of the central issues in the real debate: What transactions should be blocked? What exchanges prohibited? What exchanges priced? The market itself sheds no light whatsoever on the question of what should be traded in it. But the problem does not stop with blocked exchanges.

On what terms should things be for sale? Here the situation is even more complicated. Many "market prices" exist in a shadow cast by moral and legal considerations: I will call these *penumbral exchanges*. The *true market price* is the price that would be paid by well-informed buyers to well-informed sellers in a perfectly competitive market. Much of what can legally be bought and sold is not sold at its "true" market price.

To see how far the doctrines that we are considering are out of tune with what we actually do, consider the case of money itself. It is not sold, or better rented, at its true market price, which would be the interest rate voluntarily established between lenders and borrowers. On the contrary, interest rates are carefully managed by the Federal Reserve Board in order to stimulate employment while controlling inflation.[23] Not even research done by the Heritage Foundation or the Cato Institute is sold at its true market price since the organizations enjoy government subsidies through their tax-exempt status and nonprofit franking privileges.

Public utility prices are another prime example of prices set on the basis of criteria other than true market prices. Numerous standards other than economic efficiency, such as rights to service and avoidance of changes in the status quo, determine how prices are actually set.[24] That this is what public utility commissions actually do does not prove that this is what they should do. But it does show that, for the market disciples to be correct about pricing, all other factors must be swept aside. Gas service could be cut off to a home with small sick children. Water rates could be revised drastically if new outlying housing developments made a new reservoir a necessity. As Edward Zajac puts it, "The closer an institution is to immediate accountability, the less it will be informed by a coherent economic logic and the more by primitive notions of morality and justice."[25] Whatever the a priori logic of the market may dictate, substantial evidence exists that responsive public officials make their decisions on different grounds.

The government's agricultural policy is effected largely by incentive payments. The Soil Conservation Service, for instance, encourages farmers to engage in agricultural practices that reduce the amount of topsoil lost to erosion. The service offers both planning and financial assistance, providing an implicit subsidy to those who participate and altering the true price of farm products. If the doctrine of the Right that "free market prices must be maintained" were correct, *all* government efforts that aim at preserving agricultural resources for the future would be illegitimate.[26]

It should also be noted that churches are in the penumbra. Religious services are not delivered at their true market prices. States and localities subsidize religious institutions by exempting them from property taxes, the federal government by making contributions to religious institutions deductible. Similar arrangements exist for private schools and colleges, and the services provided by public schools and universities are obviously delivered to their students at artificially low prices. The list of penumbral prices could obviously go on and on. We need to revise our diagram again.

The result, shown in figure 5, is that the shallowness of the market failure conception of public-sector legitimacy returns to the fore. The doctrines of its proponents offer no assistance in deciding what should be in the penumbra or in deciding what the terms should be governing the transactions that take place within it. Thus, a good many other policy topics, such as

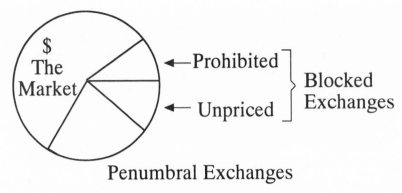

Penumbral Exchanges

Figure 5

taxation, public utility pricing, and major aspects of agricultural policy, join blocked exchanges as issues about which market theorists cannot join in real political discourse. The principle is also too strong: from their point of view, all arguments in support of blocked exchanges of either type and all penumbral exchanges must fail.

Of course, few people actually believe that everything should be for sale or that everything should be sold at its true market price, and the literature is beginning to come to grips with this issue. Market theorists might also reply that the argument that their principles are too shallow simply ignores much of what they write. Free market and centrist economists regularly discuss problems such as tax exemptions, discounting, income distribution, and the financing of education. But the adjustments to the market failure theory are ad hoc; the general, underlying principles go unchallenged, and no alternative framework is articulated.

Consider a version of market failure theory that said simply that, all else being equal, there should be a presumption in favor of the market—or, as Friedman puts it, that in making a decision we should assign extra negative weight to government intervention.[27] This is really no help at all. When we run into claims that some things should be in the penumbra and that some exchanges should be blocked, they include the presumption that all else is *not* equal. Exchanges are blocked for a variety of reasons. We cannot buy spouses, at least in part for religious reasons. Professorships of economics are not for sale because intellectual qualification, not price, is the relevant distributive criterion. Bribing public officials is prohibited because it is incompatible with democratic principles. Similar nonmarket criteria apply with respect to penumbral exchanges. A floor is put under farm prices to ensure a stable food supply. The poor cannot legally have their heat cut off in the dead of winter because society assumes a responsibility to protect the vulnerable. Churches are subsidized because of the separation of church and state: the state cannot legitimately tax churches because the power to tax is effectively the power to destroy. Saying that there should be a presumption in favor of the market simply sheds no light on the real moral issues underlying pricing and blocked exchanges.

As these examples show, our existing political structures reflect a complex political morality. We appeal to a number of criteria in making our public choices about what is to be in the market and how goods traded in the market are to be priced. Need, desert, responsibility, respect, and a vision of the good life all play roles in deciding these questions. The attempt to derive a model of government from economic analysis alone will not work. We need a full-blooded political theory that reflects our complex morality.

Once we see the role of blocked exchanges and penumbral prices, we can see clearly that *nothing* in the United States is sold in accordance with the precepts of the Right. Very large numbers of things are bought and sold. Some are very important things like food and housing in which the government intentionally intervenes. The reason that nothing is sold at its true market price is that items whose prices are controlled have effects on the prices of other things. For example, the housing subsidy that the federal government provides through the income tax deduction of mortgage interest affects the price of housing *relative* to the price of washing machines. If having a "free" market economy means governing oneself in accordance with the precepts of the Right, then the United States has no such thing. What we do have is a system closer in spirit to the "just price" conception of the Middle Ages than to the ideas of market theorists. It would be more accurate to call the American system a "Thomistic" market (after Saint Thomas Aquinas) than a "free" market, a formula that would convey the fact that our market rests on, and exhibits, a complex moral structure. The question is not, as the market devotees would have it, how we can get markets to function with perfect efficiency. It is, rather, what subsidies and other interventions in the market will serve humane and democratic purposes.

The collapse of the centrally planned Communist economies will not, we can hope, mark the advent in those countries of the "free" market as the Right sees it or the utilitarian market of the center. Our system is one of indirect central planning of supply and demand. We manage supply in numerous ways so as to affect prices in areas ranging from the land grant system of public universities, designed to make abundant and low-priced food available, to the cutting practices of the Forest Service, designed to make lumber available for houses. We manage demand with mechanisms ranging from fiscal and monetary policy to food stamps. The difference between the defunct centrally planned economies and the existing democratic regimes is thus much less sharp than is widely supposed. Over time, the industrial democracies have found that it works to manage supply and demand indirectly and centrally in order to reach democratically determined social objectives. The reaction of the West to the disaster of Speenhamland simply took a different course than that proposed by Marx, but utopian capitalism and efficient markets were discarded just the same.

WHAT WE DO

The market failure conception misjudges what is at stake. No society permits everything to be bought and sold. Indeed, things that cannot be traded for money, goods protected by blocked exchanges, are likely to be valued most. In our society, the list is long, and the list of those goods for which intentional interventions change the price, what I called *penumbral goods*, is even longer. I know of no society without blocked exchanges and penumbral goods, although obviously boundaries differ with time and place and reflect the traditions of the people in question. In a hereditary monarchy office may be awarded on the basis of birth, in a theocracy on the basis of position within the church. All stable societies succor those who are in need, although how need is understood and who has the obligation of assistance vary with time and place.

What are the considerations that give rise to the blocked and penumbral exchanges in our own society? We distribute university professorships according to demonstration of relevant expertise and public office according to fair procedures. Both processes involve merit of some sort. Food stamps and low-interest loans for education are distributed on the basis of need. Items held in the National Archives and sites of historic importance, like the Gettysburg National Battlefield, are held in trust for everyone and for the future. These last might best be called *fiduciary goods*. What we actually do with respect to fiduciary goods like these cannot be understood in terms of public goods as Friedman defines them because they easily lend themselves to exclusion. They do not fit the nonrivalness definition because they have low congestion thresholds. We could easily prevent people from

Figure 6

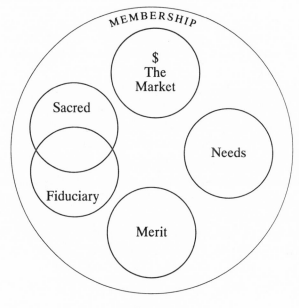

Figure 7

seeing the Constitution or from walking on the hallowed ground where Pickett charged.[28] We simply do not rely on the language of economics when we justify public expenditures on things like these.

An accurate picture of what the state should do according to the proponents of the market can be depicted again as in figure 6. There everything is conceptualized in terms of markets. The state's role is to correct for market failures. What we actually do, however, is to appeal to multiple criteria of the sort depicted in figure 7.[29] The large circle labeled *membership* indicates the boundaries of citizenship. The smaller, internal circles designate various kinds of goods. The state's job is to decide, against a backdrop of civil order and national defense and through democratic processes, the relative importance of the different spheres and to prevent the encroachment of one domain over another.

For example, it is illegal to buy public office or to obtain food stamps for reasons other than need. At least one reason why public office, for instance, is not for sale is that the arrangement would be far too dangerous. Those who bought the right to be president, subject to no review other than their checking account balance, could easily abuse their power. In our society, "sacred" goods are, at least for the most part, those having to do with the nature of persons and give rise to such laws as those that make it illegal to buy and sell children. The task of the public sector includes adjudicating between the different spheres, not reducing everything to the market.

We are now in a position to see the tragic error involved in President Reagan's Executive Order 12291, which required that the Office of Management and Budget subject all new government regulations to cost/benefit analysis. This procedure requires that we think of all activities in terms of markets in order to be able to assign prices to all costs and benefits. Once we understand the role of government as balancing between incommensurable "spheres of justice," to use Walzer's phrase, we see the futility and counterproductive nature of trying to reduce everything to the market sphere. (Of course, this is not to say that there is not a role for analyzing the cost effectiveness of various ways of reaching a goal. For example, in meeting the needs of the malnourished, it makes perfect sense to assess the relative costs of alternative plans of nutrition and distribution.)

RIGHTS, TRADITIONS, AND MARKETS

If we consider how our political discourse is actually structured, it is useful to see it as made up of three layers—rights, traditions, and markets—with a new fourth layer—the health of the biosphere—now receiving increasing attention. The language of rights comes to us from the natural law tradition through Jefferson and Locke, among others, and is embodied in constitutional government. Functionally, rights serve as claims against others for performance and thus protect us against arbitrary and capricious behavior. In nations where they are not constitutionally specified, rights may be embodied in common law. Rights function at what I will call the *foundational layer* because they are afforded strong or absolute protection by the state. In general, some of these rights may conflict with each other, but a right will trump—or take precedence over—other considerations. For example, the right to vote may not be abridged for reasons of the general welfare.

Above the foundational level there is the level of moral traditions (those traditions that are not also rights), including definitions of *merit, need, fiduciary,* and *sacred.* These are specific to a given people in a given time and place and can be understood only in that context. While rights claims can be universal, derived from attributes of human beings per se, the prescriptions of traditions acknowledge and respond to particular histories. In a just society, once rights claims are satisfied, goods are distributed according to shared understandings of these traditions.

Above the level of traditions is that of the market, the operations of which are constrained by the shared understandings of moral traditions and rights. We have seen the limitations that our culture places on the market in the lists of penumbral goods and blocked and unpriced exchanges. These constraints are derived from both levels beneath the market. The prohibition on the buying and selling of votes is derived from the level of rights. The national parks are not for sale because they are fiduciary and/or sacred goods. Food stamps are not sold by the government to everyone because they are distributed according to need.

Finally, as the environment is degraded at an accelerating rate, more and more attention is turned to the ability of the biosphere, and the ecosystems that make it up, to remain healthy enough to support human activities and to provide future generations with the productive, diverse, and beautiful world that we have enjoyed. These concerns suggest another level of constraints on the market—in a sense prior to all the rest as the precondition of survival. We can think of protecting the productivity and diversity of the biosphere as a component of protecting the rights of this and future generations. However, I conceive it separately to stress the urgency of the current situation and to reflect our duties to the biosphere as such.

The considerations derived from the levels of the biosphere, rights, and traditions lend specificity to the concepts of public goods and externalities. A depiction of how the public sector actually functions is given in figure 8. Political argument is about what belongs at what level. One seeks to locate at the lowest possible level whatever one values most dearly, for the more foundational the classification of an item, the more it is protected from the ravages of exchange. This explains the paradox that what a society values most is what it keeps from the market.

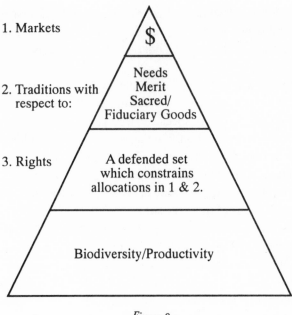

1. Markets

2. Traditions with respect to:

Needs
Merit
Sacred/
Fiduciary Goods

3. Rights

A defended set
which constrains
allocations in 1 & 2.

Biodiversity/Productivity

Figure 8

As I have shown, the defects of the centrist theory of market failures are numerous. It rests on a discredited moral theory, has little or nothing systematic to say about who gets what, has an improper account of the relations between humans and the rest of nature, does not afford an adequate account of our obligations through time, and cannot answer unavoidable questions about what should be for sale. Indeed, a more moderate literature about the uses of policy analysis has begun to appear. This literature represents, in part, a quest for an alternative, broader theory of government legitimacy in which to ground policy analysis. Works such as Hank Jenkins-Smith's *Democratic Politics and Policy Analysis* and David Weimer and Aidan Vining's *Policy Analysis* are attempts to place policy analysis in a broader political context.[30] But these works can be seen in another light, as drawing on, and in quest of, an alternative conception of government legitimacy, one such as the trust conception set out in the pages that follow.

Part II

RESTORING THE PUBLIC TRUST

And when the work of Creation was completed . . . the Lord said to the angels, "I have to place a trustee on the earth."

THE QURAN

Society is indeed a contract . . . a partnership not only between those who are living, but between those who are living, those who are dead, and those who are to be born.

EDMUND BURKE, *Reflections on the Revolution in France*

Chapter 5

THE PUBLIC TRUST

To no one will we sell, to no one will we refuse or delay right or justice.

MAGNA CARTA (1215)

The people shall be judge: for who shall be judge whether the trustee . . . acts well and according to the trust reposed in him, but he who deputes him.

JOHN LOCKE, *Second Treatise of Government*

With the failures of the dominant theory of state legitimacy in both its right-wing and centrist versions before us, we begin our quest for an adequate theory of the state, one that uses the market and other private institutions for the public good. It is not, perhaps surprisingly, a search for a new idea—but the rediscovery of an old one that has been lost to our political consciousness. This ancient idea—that the government is a trust, that those who govern are trustees—is what most of us already believe. It pulls together a progressive agenda that ranges from vaccinating our children, empowering women, and preserving our farms and forests to reorienting foreign policy toward peace and the worldwide protection of human rights. These and many other things that cry out to be done do not represent disparate or random issues of special interest groups, as the Right often charges. They are parts of a well-developed and unified progressive agenda that is waiting for an adequate theory of the state.

JOHN LOCKE AND THE PUBLIC TRUST

The idea that the government is a trustee is well grounded in our political and philosophical history, particularly in Locke's *Second Treatise of Government*, and it is Locke's conception—with one important modification—

69

that I will set forth here.[1] But the idea was not new with Locke. Its elements can be found, for example, foreshadowed in the Magna Carta and Thomas Hobbes's *Leviathan* and the Old Testament concept of the Covenant is an even more distant precursor. It was part of the general vocabulary of Locke's contemporaries as the notion of popular sovereignty gained favor, probably first appearing as an expression of the obligations of those who rule to their subjects in Poynet's *Short Treatise of Politicke Power* (1556).[2] It is carried forward in the American conservation movement by figures as diverse as Theodore Roosevelt, Gifford Pinchot, and John Muir. The idea of trusteeship was used both in the League of Nations and in the Trusteeship Council of the United Nations.

At one level, the idea of a trust is partly indeterminate. Certain duties flow directly from the notion of trusteeship, but by itself it is a fairly formal concept: we can set up a trust to preserve anything for anyone. To know in detail how governments as trustees should behave, we have to appeal to some underlying moral principles. I have used Locke's theory, for the most part as set out in the *Second Treatise*, to specify these principles and their practical consequences. My affirmative arguments in favor of the trust conception are set out in the section of this chapter entitled "Choosing the Trust Conception." Although I draw on Locke as a historical authority, my arguments stand or fall independently of the correctness of Locke's views or my interpretation of them.

Locke writes over and over again of the trust that the people repose in their government and speaks of those who govern as having a "fiduciary trust."[3] For Locke, people seek out government for the "mutual preservation of their lives, liberties and estates, which I call by the general name, property. The great and chief end, therefore, of men's uniting into commonwealths, and putting themselves under government, is the preservation of their property." In understanding Locke's theory of government, it is essential to keep in mind, as we will see, that *property* includes *life* and *liberty* as well as estate. Much of the *Second Treatise* is devoted to the circumstances under which citizens may legitimately rebel because the executive or legislator has violated the terms of the trust. The government conforms to the terms of the trust when it discharges its duties "to be directed to no other end but the peace, safety, and public good of the people."[4]

There is remarkably little disagreement as to the dominance of Locke's political philosophy in America. In *The Ideological Origins of the American Revolution*, Bernard Bailyn writes,

Referred to on all sides, by writers of all political viewpoints in the colonies, the major figures of the European Enlightenment and many of the lesser, contributed substantially to the thought of the Americans; but except for Locke's, their influence, though more decisive than that of the authors of classical antiquity, was neither clearly dominant nor wholly determinative.[5]

So, for anyone living in the United States—or other countries with a deep English heritage—the overall logic of Locke's position is very familiar. We already possess a coherent and functional conception of the role of government—even though many of us would not recognize its pedigree.

WHAT THE TRUST MODEL IS

The trust conception of government is based on the trustee's fiduciary responsibility to preserve and enhance the assets of the trust, keeping always in mind the good of the beneficiaries—in this case, the citizens. It draws on the general notion that certain persons can be given powers over certain assets to act on behalf of and for the benefit of others. Trusts are set up because there is an asset to be managed for the benefit of someone, and typically a document sets forth the duties and privileges of the trustee. Parents may place stocks and bonds in trust for their children so that the children will be financially secure in the event of the parents' death. Or one may place assets in a trust for the benefit of an institution—say a college or a home for the handicapped. The general duties of trustees are to act out of loyalty in the best interests of the beneficiary, not those of the trustee; not to delegate the entire administration of the trust; to provide the beneficiaries with information concerning the trust; to enforce claims on behalf of the trust; and to make the trust property productive.[6]

On a trust conception of government, a constitution and laws are the documents or instruments of the trust. The assets of the trust are the natural resource base, the coercive powers of the state to tax and to provide for national defense, and the state's legitimate ability to foster the well-being of both its citizens and the community as a whole. Those who govern must act in the interests of the citizens, not their own; perform the duties of office, not delegate them; disclose information to the public; defend the assets of the trust from unjust interference, destruction, or waste; and preserve and enhance the assets of the trust. The trust conception's understanding of government is, then, as follows (more specific policy implications are provided in the last three chapters).

1. *The trust conception recognizes the direct duty of the government to pre-*

serve and enhance the well-being of all persons. As beneficiaries of a trust, we expect our trustees to work for our well-being. For Locke, the state is established in order that "the law of nature be observed, which willeth the peace and preservation of all mankind."[7]

The idea that government has an obligation to preserve its citizens can be supported—and has been—in modern democratic society without explicit reference to natural law by pointing out that no one setting up a government would agree to any other rule for fear of being in an unprotected group. No one is left out, and government is charged with equal protection. The trust model thus satisfies in a direct and straightforward manner the intuitive requirement that everyone count.[8] Most proponents of the market model recognize this duty, but then claim that it can be discharged *indirectly* by relying on the market. But for those incapable of functioning in the market, those who are not Robinson Crusoes, the market approach has nothing, or at best only something ad hoc, to say.

Locke's theory also recognizes a richer conception of the person, one that crucially affects what it means for government to preserve and enhance the lives of persons. For Locke, to be a person is to be self-governing in two senses: regulating one's own conduct and choosing one's own government. This way of looking at what it means to be a person helps locate and ground a model of obligation that recognizes nonvoluntary obligations to aid the vulnerable. A person is vulnerable to the degree that she cannot be self-legislating and follow her own plans and purposes. Children are vulnerable because they are only on their way to self-governance—lacking often the self-discipline and the means to pursue their goals. The sick are vulnerable to the degree that their sickness impairs the achievement of their objectives.

As is clear from the *Letter Concerning Toleration,*[9] Locke thinks that to be a person is to be capable of setting goals, holding moral or religious beliefs, and acting on those beliefs. When Locke speaks of the trustee's obligation to preserve all persons, he refers not only to food and housing but also to the human capacity for worship and citizenship. Indeed, one of the things that worried Locke most, and a major source of his motivation in writing the *Second Treatise,* was the rise of religious intolerance and the destruction of persons both figuratively and literally because of their religious beliefs. The obligation of the trustee is thus not simply to keep people alive but to preserve their capacity as persons capable of exercising choice.

2. *The trust model holds that the legislator (and the executive) must discharge these obligations to the public good on the basis of impartial deliberation.* As Locke puts it,

Whensoever ... the legislative shall transgress this fundamental rule of society, and either by ambition, fear, folly, or corruption, endeavor to grasp themselves or put into the hands of any other absolute power over the lives, liberties, and estates of the people, by this breach of trust they forfeit the power the people had put into their hands.

The legislators must be freely chosen

and, so chosen, freely act and advise as the necessity of the commonwealth and the public good should upon examination and mature debate be judged to require. This those who give their votes before they hear the debates, and have weighed the reason on all sides, are not capable of doing.[10]

It is the obligation of legislators to debate public issues and decide on the public good in the light of that debate. Those whose votes have been committed in exchange for campaign contributions cannot, for example, discharge this obligation.

3. *The trust conception imposes an obligation to respect human rights and provides an account of those rights.* In civil society, according to Locke, persons have three clusters of rights.[11] First, there are those rights associated with democratic processes, exercised by electing representatives: "The liberty of man in society is to be under no other legislative power but that established by consent in the commonwealth." Second, rights pertaining to the integrity of the body are absolute: "Every man has property in his own person; this nobody has any right to but himself."[12] Third, there is a set of rights to some minimal level of well-being. Although Locke's theory is sometimes taken to be a justification of absolute property rights, which would preclude a government from redistributing wealth, this reading does not accord with the text.

For Locke, the "law of nature" imposes a duty on each of us to preserve humanity, including assisting the poor, or at least those incapable of working who would otherwise perish.[13] People leaving the state of nature and entering into civil government discharge their general duties for the preservation of humanity by delegating these duties to government:

The first power, viz., of doing whatsoever he thought fit for preservation of himself and the rest of mankind, he gives up to be regulated by the laws made by the society, so far forth as the preservation of himself and the rest of that society shall require; which laws of the society in many things confine the liberty he had by the law of nature.[14]

Locke's "law of nature" thus captures the idea of obligations to which we have not consented, and the social contract is the mechanism by which we

---

confer on government the responsibility to carry out those obligations on our behalf.

A more contemporary derivation of a government's duty to respect rights can avoid talking about natural law as well as other theological aspects of Locke's argument. We can see ourselves as consenting to government on the condition that it look out for our well-being as persons—keeping in mind the full-bodied sense of a person as self-legislating. Thus, individually we reserve rights against those people we ask to serve as trustees, just as beneficiaries of a financial trust have certain legal rights by virtue of their position. The golden rule—a nonvoluntary but uncontroversial source of obligation—also demands that we universalize: what we ask the government to do for us as individuals we ask it to do for all. Hence, we delegate to government the duty to treat others as we wish to be treated ourselves. The idea that we *entrust* government to act as trustee on our behalf, along with acknowledgment of the golden rule, grounds our rights along with the rights of others, as it grounds government's obligations.

4. *The trust conception explicitly prohibits waste.* A trustee's job is to conserve and enhance assets, and this has direct consequences for action. The fiduciary model recognizes that we have an obligation to leave the material resources that we find available for our use in at least as good condition as we found them in. In the *Second Treatise*, for example, Locke states that a man is entitled to appropriate from the commons whatever he has expended his labor on, "at least where there is enough, and as good left in common for others."[15] There is a duty to protect and conserve the commons for others, including future generations.

Edith Brown Weiss has developed this argument along more global lines, applying the trust conception to emerging issues of planetary management.[16] As she presents it, the fiduciary responsibility framework imposes two duties on each living generation. One is the duty of conserving options so that future generations can survive and pursue their own visions of the good life. We are obligated to preserve biological diversity, so that the benefits of a diverse gene pool will be available to our descendants, to conserve natural resources or invest in substitutes, so that we leave our descendants as many choices with respect to resources as we have had, and to preserve our cultural heritage, so that future generations can have enriched lives and learn from our mistakes and successes. The second duty is the conservation of quality, an obligation that we discharge by conserving natural resources and investing in substitutes, so that the real prices of vital resources do not rise in the future, and by conserving the unique natural

Restoring the Public Trust

resources of the world, such as places of unusual beauty, so that they can be enjoyed by our successors. The centrist version of the market model takes a bow in the direction of the former with respect to goods traded in the market insofar as it supports setting a social discount rate different from the private rate.

What bothered Locke most, in some ways, was that some people who owned potentially productive resources did not manage them for the common good. "People should be accustomed from their cradles," he argued in *Some Thoughts Concerning Education*, "to spoil or *waste* nothing at all."[17] On the fiduciary conception, waste in the management of resources can be understood in four different ways.[18] First is the overharvesting of an otherwise sustainable resource so as to destroy its capacity to sustain itself, for example, overharvesting a forest or overfishing a bay. Second, the converse, is the underharvesting of a replenishable resource, for example, letting a forest overmature to the point at which trees that could otherwise be utilized die and cannot be used commercially. (Of course, there are certain resources, those in the sacred sphere, that should not be harvested at all. This concept of waste applies only to those goods that society has decided to assign to the sphere of the market.) Third is the inefficient extraction or use of a resource, for example, by pumping oil wells at a rate that reduces the total amount that can be extracted or using water for irrigation in such a manner that much of it is needlessly lost to evaporation. Fourth is the inefficient use of a resource—using a furnace that sends unnecessarily large amounts of heat up a chimney, using a refrigerator that is poorly insulated, or driving a car that gets poor gas mileage. The government's role as trustee or steward of assets calls for policies to limit all these species of waste.

5. *The trustee must respect the virtues of commerce.* Securing a robust economy that provides for the needs of persons through trade and agriculture was one of Locke's primary concerns. Indeed, much of the *Second Treatise*, written, of course, in a preindustrial period, is devoted to developing a theory that will ensure that productive resources, particularly agricultural land, will get into the hands of those who will use them properly and well, a goal that follows directly from Locke's abhorrence of waste. In an age (similar to ours) of uncertain harvests, malnutrition, and occasional famines, one would hardly expect otherwise:

God gave the world to men in common; but since He gave it them for their benefit, and the greatest conveniences of life they were able to draw from it, it cannot be supposed He meant it should always remain common and un-cultivated. He gave it to the use of the industrious and rational (and labor was to be his title to it), not to the fancy or covetousness of the quarrelsome and contentious.[19]

But the ultimate rationale for private appropriation of the commons is that it serve the common good:

The provisions serving to the support of human life, produced by one acre of enclosed and cultivated land, are . . . ten times more, than those which are yielded by an acre of land, of equal richness, lying waste in common. And therefore he that enclosed land and has a greater plenty of the conveniences of life from ten acres, than he could have from a hundred left to nature, may truly be said to give ninety acres to mankind.[20]

As Ashcraft notes,

It is quite true that, . . . under this view, particular individuals may be able to acquire considerable wealth as the outcome of their productive and beneficial actions, but to suggest that Locke ever sets men free from their natural law obligations such that wealth may be accumulated solely because individuals desire to do so and without any social constraints on its employment is to reverse completely the thrust of his argument in the *Second Treatise*.[21]

In America, despite decades of court decisions to the contrary, the or-dinary person believes that it is self-evident that private property holders can do whatever they want with the land they own. The trust conception puts these ideas in a different and unfavorable light and suggests that there are constraints on titleholders' use of land so that the corpus of the trust is not lost or wasted. On the fiduciary conception, land is not something that can be used simply for the benefit of the present owner; rather, it is an asset that must be used for the common good understood in a multigenerational context. It is a community resource. This view is compatible with the pri-vate ownership of real property, but the rights of an owner come with the responsibilities of a steward. Indeed, for Locke, even land that has been enclosed by someone "can still be looked on as waste"[22] and can legiti-mately be taken for the common benefit if it is not effectively cultivated. Private ownership and the market have their place, but in a larger moral framework.

6. *The trust conception provides a framework for setting the obligations of foreign policy that is an alternative to the realism that has dominated Amer-ican foreign policy at least since the end of the Second World War.*[23] Nowhere does Locke limit the scope of obligations to compatriots. He talks of our

obligation to preserve all mankind, and this obligation creates a transboundary frame of reference for evaluating the conduct of other nations. Locke has essentially applied the golden rule across space: other governments have responsibilities of trusteeship, and we have obligations to help see that they are carried out.

Realist doctrines of foreign policy, however elaborate, have a simple and ancient core dogma that extends at least as far back as Thucydides' *The Peloponnesian War*. The powerful Athenians ignored the weaker Melian's plea on the grounds that "you know as well as we do that right, as the world goes, is only in question between equals in power, while the strong do what they can and the weak suffer what they must." To this the Melians made the following astonishing response: "You should not destroy *what is our common protection, the privilege of being allowed in danger to invoke what is fair and right.* . . . And you are as much interested in this as any, as your fall would be a signal for the heaviest vengeance and an example for the world to meditate upon." When the Melians failed to capitulate, the Athenians laid siege and "put to death all the grown men whom they took, and sold the women and children for slaves, and subsequently sent out five hundred colonists and inhabited the place themselves."[24] The message is clear as it can be. Unless there is a conception of law, such as Locke's natural law, for discussing what is "fair and right" in the relations between states, the strong will do whatever they will.

The trust conception provides such a framework. The foundations of the alternative to realism are twofold. The first is the stipulation in chapter 7 that "nature willeth the peace and preservation of all mankind." The second is the principle that legitimate government can be derived only from the consent of the governed. In chapter 16 ("Of Conquest") of the *Second Treatise*, Locke wrote that "conquest is as far from setting up any government as demolishing a house is from building a new one in its place."[25] Legitimate governments have obligations to their citizens, and the legitimate national governments of the world are a community of democratically elected trustees. The trustees of one nation are obligated to respect the actions of other governments with regard to the citizens of those nations. When living up to their duties as trustees, legitimate governments are to be free from interference in accord with the familiar idea of national sovereignty.

The trust conception can also be extended to a powerful critique of the behavior of nations. Trustees who abuse or neglect fiduciary obligations, for example, nations that fail to respect the human rights of their own citizens, may legitimately be held accountable by the community of nations for not discharging their responsibilities. That such a notion is current is evinced by the fact that the international community has in the past decade authorized punitive action against the oppressive white-minority government of South Africa. Such action is justified on the grounds that governments established without the consent of the governed (e.g., dictatorships) are obviously illegitimate.

The trustee conception also provides a framework for addressing the *means* by which the duties of the trustee can be enforced. Seen from this perspective, war cannot be justified simply as the continuation of the politics by other means, as the realist Clausewitz would have it.[26] Since the trustee's fundamental duty is to preserve humanity, and since war involves the intentional killing of other persons, therefore violating the fundamental spirit of trusteeship, a powerful presumption is created against war and in favor of some form of modified pacifism. Such a position does not proscribe war absolutely, however, and in the tradition of just war theory, which is compatible with and illuminated by the trustee model, can be found justification for the use of force.[27] For example, a government that is otherwise properly discharging its duties may engage in war to repel an invasion. In fact, failure to do so would be a fundamental violation of its fiduciary obligations to secure and foster the well-being of its citizens. Nevertheless, force is a last resort, to be relied on only when all other means—from sanctions, to embargoes, to blockades—have failed.

What transgressions justify international intervention in a sovereign nation's internal affairs? This question can be answered with reference to figure 8 in chapter 4, in which the importance to a society of the values plotted decreases as one moves up the diagram. The least serious transgressions are of values near the top of the triangle, the most serious of those near the bottom. A government that, for example, allows improperly regulated markets to operate, behaves foolishly but not necessarily criminally or maliciously. At the other end of the scale, when a government systematically threatens or violates the rights of its people, or when it is responsible for significant damage to the biosphere, it can be considered as having reneged on its commitment as the nation's trustee, and other governments are compelled to intervene.

For all of Locke's relevance to contemporary politics, his understanding of trusteeship is lacking in one important respect. The scope of his moral concern is limited to human beings. For Locke, "the earth and all that is therein is given to men for the support and comfort of their being."[28] Locke almost certainly has in mind here the passages from near the end of the first book of Genesis where God gives the earth and all the plants and animals to man for his use: "Have dominion over the fish in the sea, the birds in the air, the cattle, all wild animals on land, everything that creeps on the earth."[29]

One of the obvious weaknesses of this point of view is that not everything in the world is, in any direct or immediate sense, useful to human beings. More important, the findings of modern evolutionary biology suggest a quite different perspective. The burden of much of Darwin's *Descent of Man* is to argue that there is no basic difference in kind between humans and the other animals. For Darwin, humankind belongs to a community of indefinite age:

> Man with all his noble qualities, with sympathy he feels for the most debased, with benevolence which extends not only to other men but to the humblest living creature, with his god-like intellect which has penetrated into the movements and constitution of the solar system—with all these exalted powers—man still bears in his bodily frame the indelible stamp of his lowly origin.[30]

Expanding the scope of *community* in a way that takes into account post-Darwinian conceptions of who "we" are broadens the scope, but not the essential terms, of the trust. The implications of acknowledging obligations of trusteeship to other species and even ecosystems have been articulately set out by ecologist Aldo Leopold in *A Sand County Almanac*. Leopold advocates a "land ethic" that "changes the role of *Homo sapiens* from a conquerer of the land-community to plain member and citizen of it. It implies respect for his fellow members, and also respect for the community as such."[31] Of course, some of these obligations to the broader community of the biosphere will also be discharged in fulfilling the requirement to "leave enough and as good" for our descendants. Thus, there is an obvious overlap between our obligations to our own descendants and our obligations to the communities that make up the biosphere itself.

CHOOSING THE TRUSTEE CONCEPTION

Accepting the trustee model and actively applying it could transform our politics. It would give elected officials a renewed sense of mission. It would give citizens a fresh reason to expect integrity from their government and a deeper understanding of what they do when they vote. The reasons that favor the trust conception over the market model are numerous and compelling.

1. *Perhaps most obvious is that the fiduciary conception captures the idea that governments and governors have a responsibility to care for citizens.* The notion that public servants hold a trust of service that they can betray, or not live up to, is common currency in our discussions about government, but the market model can make no sense of it. In fact, the umpire model cannot even make sense of the duty of the trustee to behave carefully with the taxpayers' money! Umpires do not take care of money; trustees do. Of course, those who govern have responsibilities that go far beyond being careful with money, but the failure of the Right to capture even that financial responsibility shows the poverty of its ideas.

2. *The trust conception can help us decide what to do.* The market model's key concepts *public goods* and *externalities* are formal terms that offer little guidance for political action. The idea of trusteeship, on the other hand, points to specific spheres of activity: conserving and enhancing natural resources as assets of the trust and preserving the lives and capacities of persons. It can set the terms for deciding on things as diverse as the financing of public office, the preservation of our national parks, vaccinating our children, controlling population, and protecting the earth's ozone layer and stabilizing its climate. It helps set priorities and suggests a public agenda that reflects our deepest values.

3. *The trust conception provides a more plausible account of the means available to the state.* Umpires determine whether you are safe or out—there is no intermediate alternative. Thus, for Friedman, the choice is between the hidden hand of the market of the armored fist of government; nothing is in between markets or coercion, safe or out. But the state can and does do a variety of things between these extremes: it reminds, it assists, it educates, it cajoles and urges, it shares costs, it discovers and makes public, it holds hearings, it fines those who do not comply, etc. To extend the financial aspects of the trust metaphor, the state has a portfolio of means. A properly governed state uses all these devices to maintain order within and between the layers described in chapter 4. The trust conception helps us to see the choices that we actually have.

4. *The prescriptive conceptions of mainstream economics fit comfortably and logically under the trust conception.* These conceptions impose three duties on the trustee in areas where exchange is appropriately determined primarily by prices: to maintain competitive markets, to internalize costs, and to supply an appropriate level and mix of public goods for the benefit

of the citizens. In fact, it is only by an appeal to a satisfactory framework of political legitimacy like the trustee conception that we can decide which public goods to produce and which externalities to regulate or internalize, as shown in the discussion of the inadequacies of the market failures conception of state legitimacy. With such a background, we can achieve the full benefits of voluntary exchanges between individuals where exchange is appropriate. But we can also tell where to draw the line on the operation of the market. The trust conception can easily recognize the positive role of commerce and put it to use—as a means, but not the only means, to larger, democratically determined ends.

5. *The trust model recognizes that things are different in kind and hence embraces a vocabulary in which allocations can be understood, discussed, and balanced.* It does not even attempt the fruitless effort of reducing everything to money. As Walzer notes, in all spheres except the market, goods are distributed according to their meanings as opposed to their prices.[32] Government serves to maintain a proper balance between goods distributed on the basis of need or merit and goods that are of a sacred or fiduciary nature. A primary duty is to keep the spheres distinct and well ordered. Looking back on the Middle Ages, we can see that a theocratically based merit system held too wide a dominion. In our era, a money-based system is a primary source of disorder—penetrating spheres where distribution should be based on other criteria.[33] For example, on the trust conception, it is clear that money should not be a primary determinant of who gets public office and who gets access to those who hold public office. The umpire/market model can make no sense of this restriction.

The trust conception explicitly makes use of our moral traditions for discussing who gets what. The answers to these questions are not relegated to the realm of tastes and then dismissed. Trusteeship has a real moral vocabulary by which different kinds of goods can be understood. Need is understood in terms of descriptions of vulnerability. Merit goods are at least in large part allocated on the basis of professional competence. Fiduciary goods are preserved as a means of making the past intelligible to the present and the present intelligible to the future.

Trusteeship acknowledges the real moral claims of the needy, instead of thinking of public assistance as a way of relieving the discomfort of the rich, as Friedman would have it. Trustees must protect vulnerable persons from harm to their lives, liberty, and estates. The model thus selects against the negative income tax advocated by Friedman and in favor of programs tailored to the needs of the poor such as food stamps, housing assistance, etc. Here, again, the model fits better with what we actually do, even in conservative administrations.

The concept of trusteeship extends naturally beyond political life per se to other public positions and, in so doing, makes sense of the concepts of merit and of privilege and its attendant obligations in a way that the market model cannot. Merit controls the allocation of those goods the receipt of which requires some specific talent or qualification, for example, positions of public trust such as public office, university professorships, and the professions generally. Once attained, however, the professions are not, as Friedman would seem to have it, just another way to make money. Those who serve as professionals and enjoy the associated privileges and esteem are obligated, in exchange, to act in the public interest and observe the canons of professional ethics.[34] The state, in turn, has an obligation to see that codes of professional ethics are enforced.

Exactly how these boundaries are drawn will vary over time and from time to time become the object of renewed public discussion. For example, what we require in the way of medical education is revised periodically. But we never come close to, let alone seriously discuss, the idea that a person should be able to buy the right to be a physician. Government has a role in overseeing the professions not only to ensure that practitioners are qualified but also to ensure that barriers are not erected that either unfairly exclude some people or drive up prices.

The trust conception can also make sense of our duties to preserve fiduciary or sacred goods. Indeed, it is especially strong here, embracing Edmund Burke's notion that society is a contract between those living, those who have died, and those who will live in the future.[35] Just as we apply the golden rule in thinking about duties among nations, the trustee model applies it through time.

Rather than starting with the idea of discounting and then having to go through various machinations concerning the social discount rate in a vain attempt to arrive at a conclusion that accords with common sense, the trust conception explicitly recognizes obligations to the future. It explains the preservation of our national parks as objects of unusual natural beauty or distinction that make us aware of our connection to the broader community of nature. It allows for the protection of historic landmarks because they render the past concrete and thereby more intelligible. It even provides grounds for resisting and reversing the sale or "commodification" of such sacred places ("sacred" in the sense that they are paths to knowledge we cannot get in other ways).

Finally, the concepts of human rights are not exogenous to the trust conception as they are to the market failure theory of state legitimacy. The trust model views the traditions of and the vocabulary in which we discuss human rights as an integral part of an adequate conception of the role of the state. With the Burkean historical perspective built into the trust model, the origins and changing character of our rights are an intelligible and necessary portion of a public philosophy of governance.

6. *The fiduciary conception has the capacity to address the special crises of natural resources and biostability with which we are faced in the late twentieth century.* Market theorists, arguing that the market will ensure the efficient use of resources and generate alternatives, and concentrating on aggregate supply, have held that scarcity is no longer a problem. Cornucopians like Julian Simon have made much of the fact that, for instance, the proven reserves of many resources such as fossil fuels continue to increase or at least remain constant in the face of *rising* use while real prices are steady or falling.[36] They point to the market as a fantastic creator of wealth that since the end of the Middle Ages has generated unprecedented levels of income for large numbers of people. It has helped replace, especially in Europe, a world in which there were chronic shortages of necessities with a world of surpluses.

Indeed, agricultural surpluses now plague the developed world, and many nations have explicit programs to reduce the amount of land that is farmed. If widespread food shortages should recur, this excess capacity can be tapped or a portion of the grain fed to livestock diverted. (In years of small harvests, the market tends to make this allocation itself by increasing the price of grain, thus causing livestock owners to reduce the amount of grain fed per animal or the number of animals, or both.) Also, as the techniques of modern competitive agriculture take hold in parts of the former Soviet Union, it is probable that the output of these regions will grow much greater, perhaps even showing a surplus, although whether and when this will occcur is by no means certain.

Despite the successes of the market, waste is still a fundamental issue that must be addressed by political theory. For example, food, water, and clean air are scarce for many people right now. The number of people in the world who are malnourished is between 350 million and 1 billion. Water for drinking, bathing, and irrigation is chronically short in many places. Air pollution is so severe in many Third World cities as to be a major factor in ill health.[37] Because people like Friedman and Simon have little to say about distributive justice, their fascination with the aggregate success of the market blinds them to such ongoing violations of the terms of the trust. The trustee model, on the other hand, makes it a central concern by insisting on preserving lives.

The most honest answer to the question of whether the world is about to enter a *global* crisis in the supply of food or some other natural resource would seem to be no. Not in the next decade. And perhaps not in the decade following that. But this does not mean that Malthus may not ultimately be right. The human population may outrun the food supply, although there is no evidence that we are near that threshold yet. Will there be severe shortages of the natural resources necessary to run a modern economy in the middle of the next century? Here, an honest answer can be only that we just do not know. Projections of the size of future human populations could be off by several billion in either direction. We do not know what the rate of technological innovation will be; hence we do not know what substitutes for resources that would otherwise be in short supply will be found.

But, whatever the future holds, there is now a new kind of scarcity. The very success of industrialized market economies is leading to a scarcity of ecological diversity and stability and of coherent human communities. Indeed, the problem in some dimensions is not that we *will* run out some of the basic inputs of industrialized economies in the intermediate term but that we *will not*. Ecological diversity and stability are severely threatened around the globe in a variety of ways, including habitat destruction for housing and commercial development, the harvesting of forest products, nonsustainable agriculture, the introduction of exotic species, and pesticides. But the fundamental threats, causing unprecedented biospheric disequilibrium, are the growth in the human population, the release of heat-trapping gases that are the by-products of economic activity, and the thinning of the earth's protective ozone layer.

Perhaps the ultimate failure of the market model is its failure to take into account the fact that the economy is dependent on the biosphere. Suppose that we did everything in accordance with the market model as presented by Friedman or by the more promising tradition of the center: markets would be competitive, the proper mix of public goods supplied, and all externalities internalized. This still leaves unaddressed the question of whether the resulting mix of human economic activity can be sustained by the biosphere on which it depends, a question central to the trustee conception.

7. *In recognizing our unavoidable interdependence, the trust conception rests on a more plausible account of our moral obligations.* Trusteeship places

concern for the well-being of people, especially the vulnerable, at the center of government responsibility. Caring for each other is something that is unavoidable, not an anomaly to be explained in an otherwise self-interested model. We should see the unproblematically independent Robinson Crusoe, not as a major figure in a theory of the state, but simply as an intriguing fiction. Interestingly, however, the Crusoe analogy has an indirect use within the trust conception: to the degree that people are *not* like Robinson Crusoe, we should be alert to our obligations of assistance.

What is at stake can best be captured by what Robert Goodin has called the vulnerability model of obligations.[38] In this conception, our fundamental responsibility is to forestall threatened harms to one another. The vulnerability model does a better job than the voluntaristic model not only of explaining how our obligations arise but also of explaining what those obligations are. On the voluntaristic model, I am obligated to do what I have agreed to do, but I am given no guidance as to what it is that I should agree to do. The vulnerability model fills in the details. If, for example, my spouse is sick, I should see that she receives appropriate medical care, sympathy, and my assistance in recovery. In other words, my obligation is to reduce her vulnerability. Even if I did not promise explicitly to aid and comfort, I would still be obligated. The vulnerability model also extends to strangers as well as family, friends, or neighbors, people to whom we are not linked by contract or promise. We may not, justly, pass by those outside our immediate community when they are in need. Their vulnerability and our ability to help obligate us. At the same time, our obligations do not extend to exhausting all our resources in assisting others or to forgoing our own journey, an insight captured by the New Testament story of the Good Samaritan.

Indeed, even Friedman's account of when the government can legitimately intervene in the market can be explicated, at least in part, in terms of vulnerability.[39] On a voluntaristic account, all our obligations depend on promises. But what is it about a promise that creates an obligation in the first place? Suppose that I make a promise in a letter that is permanently lost in the mail. No one ever knows about it, so no one relies on it. Compared to promises on which other people depend, this promise has little force, perhaps none. The more others have ordered their lives on the basis of what we have said, the more we are obligated to keep our word to them. This is to say that our obligation comes out of their vulnerability to harm that arises out of the expectations that we have created. The right of the state to enforce contracts—which Friedman recognizes—derives from the fact that others have relied on what the contract says; thus, vulnerability undergirds our commitment to contracts.

In fact, this analysis also applies to Friedman's other justifications for government interference in the market: the necessity of dealing with monopolies and with externalities. One of the most undesirable things about monopolies is that they exploit those dependent on their services, garnering extra profits. It is precisely the power wielded by the monopoly that makes individuals vulnerable to exploitation. We rely on government regulation to keep monopolies from forming and amassing such power. If we allow a technical monopoly to develop (e.g., the phone company), we regulate it heavily to prevent exploitation of vulnerable customers. Services must be available to all without discrimination; services cannot be cut off without warning; rates and profits are both set by public commissions, not by market decisions. Regulation of monopolies explicitly recognizes the argument of vulnerability.

Negative externalities, or neighborhood effects, as Friedman calls them, are costs to society that are not included in regular market decisions. The industrialist who pollutes the river does not count the costs to the citizens downstream. Citizens are vulnerable to this type of exploitation because the effects on each person may be small and ignored. The acknowledgment that government might have an obligation to correct for externalities is best seen as a response to this threat of harm without efficient recourse. Thus, even the exceptions to the free market structure endorsed by Friedman can be seen as being justified at least in part because of the way they address essential human vulnerabilities.[40] In fact, these arguments explain why government does these things more readily and more fully than Friedman's own account does. When we acknowledge vulnerability as a source of obligation, we see that government's responsibilities go far beyond correcting market failures.

Once we look at the obligations of the state in terms of the vulnerability conception, the idea of equality—often cited as a goal of progressive government—becomes less important. It is not the obligation of the state to reduce inequality per se but the responsibility to protect its citizens from harm that lies behind progressive politics. Inequality is relevant only if it is a direct cause of vulnerability. The fact that we have instituted in-kind transfers such as food stamps, housing vouchers, and Medicaid, as opposed to simple transfers of income, demonstrates that the root idea at work in our tradition of entitlement programs is vulnerability, not equality of income. Having never raised expectations concerning equality of results, the trust conception avoids the paradoxes involved in the debate about achieving it.

8. *The trust conception can make sense of the virtues of citizenship.* Surprisingly, it can provide a rationale for the conservative virtue of patriotism that the conservatives' own model of the state cannot. Since the state is explicitly charged with advancing our well-being, loyalty to it, loving it, and identifying with it are not mysterious feelings to be explained away. Rather, they are quite natural expressions toward an entity that protects us and of which, through democratic processes, we are a part. In those rare circumstances in which international conflict is justified, this is a state to which one could understandably give that "last full measure of devotion."

Indeed, the trust conception is generally robust with respect to the duties of citizenship, those that attach to our public lives together.[41] The government is created and sustained by the consent of the citizens, who are obligated to participate in the process of government. This in turn creates an obligation to be literate and informed so as to ensure meaningful participation in democratic processes. It requires honesty so that the debate will not be misleading and choice thus undercut. When we see ourselves as members of a community that stretches backward and forward in time, we can see that we ourselves are stewards: of land and the diversity and productivity of the earth generally, of capital, of our religious, moral, and cultural heritage. The virtues of saving and frugality are central duties of the citizen. We work in cooperation with government in the discharge of these sacred duties to our children and our children's children.

9. *Finally, the trust conception is comprehensive since it contains an account of our obligations both through time and across space.* Most contemporary theories of the state provide no account of what we owe to noncompatriots, persons who live outside our borders. But this cannot be satisfactory for two reasons. First, while theories of the nation-state assume that duties of justice stop at national borders, most accounts of morality refer to duties to all persons. Second, as the world becomes more and more interconnected, there is even less reason than there ever was to believe that the effects of our actions stop at the border.

Once we see that traditional accounts of state legitimacy are unsatisfactory if they assume that duties stop at borders, it is an easy step to see that they are also inadequate if they limit obligations to contemporaries. The results of our actions are no longer confined to the present—if, indeed, they ever were. One of the great strengths of the trustee model is that it gives an explicit account of our duties to the unconceived. Most theories of state obligation simply ignore the issue.

DEFENDING THE TRUST CONCEPTION

The trust conception presents an alternative vision to current ways of thinking about domestic politics and international relations. It is, however, tempting to dismiss it as a utopian scheme—desirable, but unworkable. The market model in both its Right and its centrist version, for example, contains an account of how the self-interested motivation of private individuals can work for the common good through exchange. Those who govern are pursuing their own interests in holding public office, and their primary task is to keep markets working so that the pursuit of self-interest will serve the public interest.

From this perspective, the trust conception appears to lack a theory about how to motivate the trustee. Indeed, it appears to require actions that cannot be motivated. Here, as elsewhere when the self-interest hypothesis is invoked, it is vital not to concede the initial dichotomy between self-interest and altruism. An institution founded solely on altruism would be unstable at best. Rather, it is better to recast the question as, Which self do I want to serve? Assuming a role creates new self-definitions, new identities. One way to understand the motivation of the trustee is to compare her to other familiar professionals. Physicians are supposed to place the well-being of patients ahead of their own interests, and we have no problem condemning doctors who put their own interests first, such as those who refer their patients to their own diagnostic centers. The issue is how we get professionals to interpret their self-understanding in a way that stresses the duties built into their role.

The trustee acts in the public interest because she accepts the obligations that her role confers. Those who seek public office, either elected or appointed, are motivated by honor—by the approbation of their fellows. And we pay them homage as a way of reinforcing—we hope—their integrity. Perhaps it would make economists happy to refer to this homage as the price we pay to ensure such integrity. (Note that even Friedman would implicitly have to rely on at least some conception of impartial choices by people in government, say, in awarding defense contracts, to make even his minimal state work, so the trustee model bears no special burden in this regard.)

Another class of objections might hold that, in a variety of ways, the trust model requires too much: that it is too disruptive of our individual lives and plans, requiring as it does excessive concern with the preservation of others. It is startling, however, to note that the other-regarding aspects of the trustee conception are extremely modest when compared to the underlying moral assumptions of market-based models. The centrist market model finds its roots in classical utilitarianism, whose defects we considered in chapter 4. Recall that utilitarianism requires that we seek the greatest happiness of the greatest number. The market school accepts this obligation and then falsely claims that obligations can be discharged indirectly through voluntary exchanges. Note how strong the requirement is that *happiness* be maximized. It requires that our own projects and purposes always be subject to revision or cancellation if we could thereby achieve greater happiness overall. If we are seeking a more modest account of our obligations to others, the trustee's concern with only the *preservation* of all is preferable by far. Ironically, the centrist market account, which can seem so selfish, is, at bottom, altruistic in the extreme.

While the obligation to preserve all persons might seem especially demanding and disruptive once we recognize its global implications, the underlying duty of preservation is first of all an obligation of national governments. Our individual obligations are properly discharged indirectly, through the governments of the world, the community of trustees.[42] The citizens of one nation have duties to those of another only when the other government does not or cannot discharge its duties. Trustees do have the conventional duties of aid when local resources are overwhelmed by natural disaster, civil strife, and the like, but their primary international duty is to work for a just world order under which the rights of all people are satisfied by their own governments. Except for responding to natural disasters, in a just and well-ordered world we could legitimately attend only to compatriots.

This may be dismissed by realists as utopian. In the real world, which is in part a result of an absence of coherent normative principles for governing international relations, the problem routinely arises of how to deal with noncomplying states—international rogues. But, as the twentieth century draws to a close with more than 100 million persons dead as a result of war, it is the realists' position that must be seen as infeasible.

In the context of the trustee conception, other nations' response to governments that do not discharge their duties properly should—adopting the principles outlined by Thoreau for individuals in *Civil Disobedience*, at least in the first stages—be nonviolent noncooperation.[43] Because of the inter-penetrating nature of the world economy and the growing movement to guarantee basic human rights worldwide, nonviolent, moral suasion should have more force than in the past. Of course, for nonviolent means to succeed, it is important that nations not have vast armies at their disposal, making arms control vital. Force should be used to deal with noncompliance only if it will save lives in the long run, although Thoreau might not have been comfortable with even this exception. In any event, it is hoped that a show of force will on the whole be sufficient.[44]

It might be objected, on the other hand, that the trustee model permits too much, that, for example, it asserts so many duties that it paves the way for a large bureaucratic state and unwarranted intervention in the lives of the citizens. This objection is, however, without force with respect to either means or ends. The trust conception does not place our civil and religious liberties in jeopardy—these rights are built into it from the beginning. In cases of conflict between the will of the people, as expressed through the legislature, and rights, rights trump.

The objection also ignores the many means available to the trustee. The model does not, for example, condemn the market. Indeed, one of the duties of the trustee is to ensure that markets operate efficiently once we know what public goods to produce and which externalities to control. Trusteeship does not demand a return to large public bureaucracies. Having a duty to use the taxpayer's money with care, it is perfectly pragmatic and moves in the direction of parsimonious government. Hence, the trustee should discharge its fiduciary duties in the most effective manner possible. As we will see in the following chapters, it can readily rely on tax incentives, on privatization of public services, or on market-oriented demand subsidies should these steps discharge its responsibilities most efficiently.

The trustee conception is not radically egalitarian, favoring large income or other resource transfers for their own sake. While the concept *preserving all mankind* recognizes the moral worth of all persons, it does not command us to provide each person with equal monetary income. There are clear obligations *to* the poor because of their vulnerability and clear limits on those obligations. There are also clear obligations *of* the poor to remain productive members of society and to share in the obligations of citizenship.

Ironically, it is the market model in both its Right and, to a lesser extent, its centrist versions that permits too much, both by government and by individuals. In assuming that our obligations to one another can be discharged through mutually self-interested exchange, it contains no account of what we owe our contemporaries at home or abroad; nor does it provide a satisfactory account of our obligations to future generations. In failing to recognize, much less deal with, the dependence of the economy on the biosphere, the market model legitimates the destruction of the broader community of life of which we are a part.

The trust model lies at the center of our tradition of political theory, but it has disappeared from the political arena. In the chapters that follow, ways of thinking are set out that can give us and our politicians new ways of talking about what "government of, by, and for the people" can and should do.

Chapter 6

RESTORING GOVERNMENT AND PRESERVING PERSONS

There is on earth a thing two-footed and four-footed and three-footed, which has one voice . . . but when it goes on most feet, then its speed is feeblest.

SOPHOCLES, *Oedipus Rex*

The trust conception is not merely a theory that helps us think fruitfully about government in a general way, although it is that. It is also a guide to policy and politics, a guide to action. And it generates specific results. It exhibits, underlines, and gives coherence and historical legitimacy to a progressive political agenda that otherwise appears fragmented and disconnected. As I will show in chapter 8, it can provide a foundation for thinking about how we should pay for these government programs.

In this and the next chapter, I show how the trust conception helps set priorities. The requirement of impartiality will show why we need to change the way elections are financed. The trustee's duty to protect the vulnerable will generate a far-reaching social agenda. The idea that to be a person in the full sense of the word is to be self-governing shows the way to education reform and the control of substances that impair or destroy choice. Recognizing our responsibility to people beyond those in our immediate community puts foreign policy and national defense in new contexts with different priorities.

In what follows, the policies that I outline are not fully developed, meant only to show the general direction taken by a government grounded by the trust conception. A different understanding of the facts in a particular area may generate disagreement over specific recommendations. If, however, we accept the trust conception as an overall framework for government legitimacy, then we should be able to resolve those disagreements insofar as we can agree on what the facts are.

RESTORING THE INTEGRITY OF PUBLIC OFFICE

Above all, we must restore the legitimacy of our governmental institutions, or our common destiny will continue to be subject to the vagaries of private interests. The central idea of the trust conception is that the trustee, the government, must act to promote the interests and values of the beneficiaries, the citizens, impartially. If it does not, everything else is placed at risk. Nothing may legitimately be done that would diminish the ability or inclination of the trustee to discharge his or her obligations impartially. Thus, how the trustee is selected is perhaps the point on which a government turns.

Seen from this perspective, the present system, under which campaign financing comes predominantly from political action committees (PACs), at least for House and Senate races, is illegitimate. In essence, PACs buy the votes of those members of Congress whom they support and thus expect to promote their political and social agenda. In the 1990 elections, for example, political action committees contributed $94 million to individuals running for seats in the House, the vast majority of that money ($87 million) going to incumbents. (Nonincumbents received only $7 million in 1990.)[1] "Soft money"—money contributed privately to state party organizations (which are not covered by federal laws) in order to promote candidates in federal elections—also compromises the impartiality of federal lawmakers, who understand their debt not to voters but to patrons.[2] The temptation to sell one's impartiality for the sake of reelection is everywhere and is surely a significant factor in the public's disaffection with government generally. Thanks, de facto, to the pervasiveness of the market model, political offices are now for sale and the actions of the officeholders suspect.

Four policies—none of them now in place—would counteract the current commodification of and inequality of access to public office. First, campaign contributions should be eliminated altogether or capped at a very low level, whether they come from PACs or from private individuals. Second, it should be illegal to use funds given to a state political party not covered by federal election reform to influence a federal election by any means, including getting out the vote on election day. Third, to mitigate the inequality between wealthy (often very wealthy) candidates for office and all others, a cap should be placed on campaign spending. Fourth, in order to reduce the private cost of running for public office, public funding should be provided for all candidates who secure votes or signatures at some significant level, a policy implemented now only for presidential elections. Also along these lines, because the current system unfairly favors incumbents, most of whom are white men, special attention should be directed to devising funding arrangements that empower women and people of color—perhaps a special fund provided by the political parties that would serve to supplement the funds available from the federal government.

It will be objected that these proposed reforms interfere unduly with the liberty that people should have to spend their money as they wish—that they interfere with freedom of speech. But it is not difficult to ground these reforms even on Friedman's principles, which stressed—as one of the principal arguments in favor of capitalism—the importance of separating economic and political power.[3] In fact, we have already accepted substantial limitations in the case of presidential elections. Trusteeship requires that we continue the project.

PROTECTING THE VULNERABLE

Not only does the trust conception provide clear prescriptions about removing public office from the realm of the marketplace, but it also provides clear guidelines for what those who hold office should do. By focusing on our duty to protect the vulnerable, the model reveals the problems that afflict the poor as interconnected social and personal failures and allows the development of mutually reinforcing public aid programs. Addressing vulnerability does not necessarily mean a return to the large bureaucracies supporting massive public hospitals, housing projects, and the like. Such interventions as federally administered medical insurance, housing vouchers, and food stamps are likely to discharge these obligations effectively. Nor, given Locke's abhorrence of idleness, does the model preclude requiring work (from those who can)—and socially responsible conduct in general—as a condition of public assistance. In fact, the trust conception can guide us toward appropriate and effective government intervention in a wide variety of sensitive social issues—ranging from caring for our children to gun control.

Children. Our children are quite literally the future of our culture, our nation, and our species. Under the trust conception, we have at least three

---

Restoring the Public Trust

classes of partially overlapping duties to them. Children are clearly among the most vulnerable members of society, and it is our duties to them in that regard that are discussed here. Protecting the productive capacity and diversity of the environment, also a duty we owe to our children, is discussed in the next chapter. Our duty to see that they grow up to be productive members of society is discussed below in connection with education and family planning.

The final report of the National Commission on Children, created by Congress in 1987, summarized the now familiar dismal statistics about our nation's children:

> One in four children is raised by just one parent. One in every five is poor. Half a million are born annually to teenage girls who are ill prepared to assume the responsibilities of parenthood. An increasing number are impaired before birth by their parents' substance abuse. Others live among violence and exploitation, much of it fueled by a thriving drug trade. Rich and poor children alike face limited futures when their educations are inadequate and they have few opportunities for cultural enrichment and community service. Too many children at every income level lack time, attention, and guidance from parents and other caring adults. The result is often alienation, recklessness, and damaging, antisocial behavior.[4]

When we compare the status of our children with that of those of other nations, the results are shocking. The Children's Defense Fund has noted that American children are more likely to die in their first year of life than children in eighteen other countries, are less likely to be immunized against polio in infancy than children in sixteen other nations, are far more likely to be poor than children in many other industrial countries, lag behind the children of many other nations in education, and have far higher teenage pregnancy rates.[5]

Under the fiduciary conception, there are clear public responsibilities to improve and protect the lives of our children on all these fronts.[6] We would at least be on our way to meeting our duties as trustees if we followed the recommendations of the majority report of the National Commission on Children, which presents a comprehensive approach to improving the status of our children. It advocates a national health service corps to provide health care in underserved areas, special support for high-risk students, improved child-care programs, and related policies.

Some programs have proved especially and consistently effective and can therefore serve as models and an inspiration. First, all children should be vaccinated against a range of diseases by the age of two. Clinics could be set up in cities and towns to give free vaccinations, or vouchers could be provided for parents to present to private physicians. Exactly what form these measures take will depend on how a national health insurance policy (discussed below) evolves. Parents, as trustees in their own right, would still be obliged to secure the vaccinations, and failure to do so would qualify as a form of child neglect and therefore open the way for legitimate state intervention. Net savings to the public sector would result from this program alone since it is significantly less expensive to prevent diseases than to treat them. In this case, our duties to protect the vulnerable and to use public revenues effectively go hand in hand.

Second, the Women, Infants, and Children (WIC) program should be fully funded for all 7 million Americans now eligible (approximately 4 million are served now).[7] This exceptionally cost-effective program provides prenatal care to poor pregnant women and food and preventive health care to their children, reducing or even eliminating the expense of treating later health problems that are due to early deprivation. To increase its effectiveness, WIC should be integrated with a program of family planning services provided by a national health insurance scheme. It will also prove more successful if it is coupled with efforts to reduce some of the maternal behaviors associated with low birth weight and malnutrition, such as smoking and the abuse of alcohol.[8]

Third, Head Start should be made available to all the 2.5 million children who are eligible, not just the approximately 600,000 children served, for example, in 1990.[9] Head Start provides preschool-aged children from poor families with the educational opportunities they need to succeed in grade school and beyond. Despite recent efforts to downplay the program's success, the data documenting its effectiveness are positive, although some program redesign is in order.[10] Children who have participated in this program are more likely to perform well in school than nonparticipants with similar backgrounds, and these gains generally persist. In addition, children in Head Start programs generally receive better health care services, and the program has a favorable influence on the career paths of their parents.[11]

Finally, both the Children's Defense Fund and the National Commission on Children recommend that all families with children receive a tax credit. The commission sets the rate at $1,000 per child.[12] The basic idea is that the government should not tax away the money that it takes to raise a child, thus undercutting parents' ability to discharge their duties as trustees.

National Health Insurance. A health insurance scheme that provides all citizens with a basic package of medical services is required to satisfy the government's obligation to protect the well-being of its citizens. The more than 30 million Americans without any health insurance coverage are vulnerable to harm in an especially urgent way, and the trust model imposes a clear obligation on the government to rectify this situation. The trustee may not legitimately sit idly by while uninsured beneficiaries of the trust die in the halls of emergency rooms.

At the time of this writing, a great variety of plans are under consideration, two examples among which stand out. One exceptionally comprehensive study of the current system and its defects, the so-called Pepper Commission Report, issued its recommendations in September 1990.[13] The Pepper plan would require that every American be provided with health insurance, either by an employer or by the government. Employers who found private markets too expensive could purchase insurance directly from the federal government, which would specify a minimum benefits package. A variety of cost control mechanisms would include assessments of effective treatments, consumer payment of part of the costs of services, managed care to assure that cost-effective treatment is pursued in complex cases, and more efficient ways of paying providers. Preventive care for those over the age of sixty-five would be strengthened, and those with incomes less than twice the poverty line would receive special financial assistance.

Henry Aaron of the Brookings Institution has proposed what he calls the "universal-access single-payer health plan." Aaron summarizes the plan as follows: "In brief, the . . . plan would provide essentially universal financial access to acute care. It would greatly expand access to long-term care. And by creating constrained entities that are empowered to negotiate fees and hospital budgets, it would establish the basis for control over the growth of medical care costs."[14] The plan would require that all employers offer health insurance directly through private suppliers or pay the government a premium for coverage. Those not connected with the work force would have coverage with some capped benefits provided directly by the government. Because this plan would dramatically expand the number of "bidders" in the market for health care, cost control is a key issue. To deal with the problem of rising costs in the health sector, a system of "financial agents" in different regions of the country would be empowered to control costs and to pay suppliers.

It must be recognized, however, that some inequalities in health care are unavoidable in any society like ours that organizes its economic activities around a market and pays different salaries for different jobs. In such a society, one of the rewards of middle- and high-income status is the ability to buy more and more varied things, including medical care. Inevitably, under any plan with set, but limited, benefits, some people will be able to afford health care that others cannot. The trustee conception requires a floor to be built beneath the vulnerable, not uniformly similar provisions for all. But this limited inequality should not be seen as a reason for blocking otherwise progressive comprehensive plans. And, of course, any national health insurance program should include family planning and health care for both mother and child.

National Housing Assistance Program. Many Americans are homeless, many live in housing that is inadequate, and many are forced to pay too great a share of their income for housing. Clearly, our trustees are not here discharging their obligation to protect the vulnerable. Efforts on the part of government to build and operate housing have, for the most part, failed dismally, and in some cases these costly structures have had to be destroyed because people simply would not live in them. It seems much more effective to intervene on the demand side. A system of housing certificates would allow renters and developers alike to exercise choice in the market, relieving the government of the obligation of building and operating the housing stock itself. Such a system should include a requirement for self-help, meant to reduce dependency, that would terminate assistance to certain classes of recipients after some time period.

Firearms. A fundamental obligation of a government is to protect the lives of its citizens. The Reagan/Bush administrations violated this fundamental obligation by failing to back, and actually vetoing, curbs on the availability of weapons that now kill over 23,000 Americans a year. In 1990, 10,567 people in the United States were murdered with handguns—a figure up 11 percent from 1989. In a typical year, over 11,000 people use handguns to commit suicide, and about 1,600 are killed in handgun accidents. In 1988, handguns were used to murder nineteen people in Sweden, eight in Canada, and 8,915 in the United States. (Both Canada and Sweden have strict laws controlling handguns.)[15] Automatic and semiautomatic weapons (some of which can fire over 1,000 rounds a minute) are regularly used on the streets of many of our cities and increasingly in the suburbs as well. More and more people are killed or injured by random bullets, sometimes while in their own homes. Many areas of our country are best described as being in a state of anarchy.

Guns are not, as the Right would have it, just another commodity to be bought and sold. No moral or constitutional right exists entitling a private citizen to own something primarily for the purpose of killing other people. The Constitution clearly puts the right to bear arms in the context of a public militia. Two uses follow from this context. One is the ability to raise an army to repel an invader. The other is to keep alive the possibility of a revolution in the event that the government itself becomes oppressive. In an age of tanks, laser-guided missiles, and the like, however, it is sheer fantasy to suppose that guns in the hands of the citizenry will be effective in defeating the military forces controlled by modern governments, whether foreign or domestic.

The trust conception requires that we take radical, but from its point of view commonsensical, steps to stop the slaughter resulting from the current widespread possession by private citizens of handguns and other firearms. It should be against federal law for a private citizen to own any handgun for any purpose. Because there will almost certainly be widespread non-compliance with any strict handgun law in its early phases, such a ban should be coupled with a ban on the manufacture, shipment, sale, or use of all handgun ammunition and the materials to make such ammunition.[16] It should be against federal law for a private citizen to own any rifle or shotgun that is, or can readily be made, fully or semiautomatic. Only firearms with bolt, lever, or pump actions and breech loading capacities appropriate for hunting and sport shooting should be legal. (For reasons that will be explored more fully below, hunting is a necessary evil under the trust conception because of the need to control the ecological imbalances introduced by the elimination of natural predators.)

It will be important to create incentives for compliance with these laws, and both "carrots" and "sticks" are available. During a grace period of, say, five years, guns of historic value could be dedicated to museums in exchange for a tax deduction, which would be based on the guns' market value prior to the ban on private ownership. The federal government should offer to buy other guns—a program that has been tried at the local level.[17] Local, state, and federal law enforcement officers should increase their attention to the issues of compliance with gun control laws. At the end of the grace period, penalties should be emphasized. Stiff mandatory prison terms should be required for those not in compliance, and even stiffer penalties should attach to the use of a firearm in any crime. We need not be deterred by the tautological bumper sticker that states, "When guns are outlawed, only outlaws will have guns." The Right, which customarily claims that the main way to control any crime is through deterrence, is hardly in a position to claim that that very deterrence will be ineffective only in the case of firearms. Nor is the control of firearms an undue interference with the liberties of citizens. It follows quite simply from the government's obligation not to allow citizens to harm one another. Indeed, we can even appeal to Friedman's principle that the government has a duty to maintain law and order, thus revealing that his own system may be grounded in the vulnerability model, a foundation Friedman does not see.

FOSTERING AND PRESERVING CHOICE

An integral part of Locke's concept of a person is the idea of the individual as citizen and entrepreneur. Citizens are capable of governing themselves and deliberating about their goals and the public good, hold certain moral and religious beliefs that inform these judgments, and are capable of making their way in the world of commerce. But, while relying on this understanding of a person, the trust conception also makes it clear that the existence of such self-aware and competent citizens cannot be taken for granted. One of the trustee's duties to its beneficiaries is to foster full-blooded personhood in this sense.

Education for Citizenship and Commerce. It is the job of the government to see to it that all its citizens receive a proper and sufficient education. Of course the basic skills—literacy and numeracy—are a necessity. Children should also be trained in the manual and symbolic skills that they will need to attain economic self-sufficiency. And along with these skills should go a thorough grounding in the moral virtues on which capitalism depends: hard work, which is required for a productive economy; thrift, which is necessary for the formation of capital; and truthfulness, on which contracts depend. Education should ultimately foster the virtues of democratic citizenship: fidelity to law motivated by internalized norms, not by fear of state reprisal; an insistence on truth telling on the part of the citizens; and a disposition on the part of the citizens to require truthfulness from the trustee. One of the tragic ironies of Friedman's umpire conception of government is that it cannot account for the role of the government in creating the skills and virtues necessary in a contemporary capitalist society.[18] Umpires do not educate or train players. Looked at from the fiduciary perspective, responsible capitalism and democracy do go hand in hand; they depend, however, not on free markets, but on free and self-governing men and women.[19]

Public education should be the principal vehicle for providing this proper and sufficient education. Parents should be free to send their children to private schools if they so choose—and if they can afford to. But the recently proposed voucher systems—attempts to introduce market mechanisms into the realm of education—are for two reasons inherently suspect. The first derives from the trustee's role in preserving culture. A functional civilization needs to have common values (liberal virtues if you like), a core set of beliefs that constitute the foundations of acceptable behavior.[20] Citizens as stewards need to have a shared understanding of history and literature to know what culture or cultures they hold in trust. Hence we are led, perhaps, in the direction of making English the national language or of requiring that all citizens receive a bilingual education. Those voucher schemes that emphasize a common set of values and a common curriculum are not objectionable from this point of view, at least on a priori grounds, but then how they differ from the public school system is less clear as well. Second, if voucher schemes are available to all parents regardless of income, the difference between the education received by rich and poor children will increase as rich parents' ability to purchase a better education increases. Poor children will therefore be worse off than before and more vulnerable to the vicissitudes of the labor market.

Family Planning. Among the most important means of guaranteeing self-governing citizens is assuring that every child is truly wanted, that all children experience the love and nurture that make it possible for them to have self-respect as adults.[21] A straightforward way of increasing the likelihood that children are truly wanted is to enable parents to understand and control their fertility. We need to assure that potential parents understand the consequences of the exercise of their sexuality. There should be federally mandated universal reproductive education in the schools beginning at slightly before the age of puberty and continuing through the end of high school. This education should include material on the social as well as the biological aspects of reproductive behavior. The education, career, and income consequences of teenage pregnancy must be clear to all teenagers, especially girls, who are often trapped in poverty by an early pregnancy. All teenage boys should be made well aware of the tough new child-support laws and of the costs of supporting a child until the age of majority. Above all, these laws must be enforced.

An important study has found that, in comparison with other Western countries, the manner in which birth-control services are delivered in the United States fails to support "the promotion of the modern, highly effective methods of contraception. In addition, there appears to be a lack of readily available information about contraceptive methods and services in the United States, especially simple, objective messages in the mass media."[22] At a minimum, condoms should be available free of charge to all high school students in the United States—as they already are in many areas in response to the AIDS epidemic.[23] To counter the nearly total lack of research on birth control in the United States, the federal government should initiate a special program under the auspices of the National Institutes of Health.[24] The results of this research should be in the public domain so that any company wishing to develop products based on its findings could do so without a patent. If companies continue to withhold products from the market because of fears of liability, the government should produce and market the products itself. Birth-control information should be disseminated through nonprovocative advertisements and programming on radio and television and also available through the national health insurance program.

It will be objected that sex education in the schools and public involvement in family planning involve an undue intrusion into moral and religious issues, better left to the family. This can be countered on a number of grounds. The present system of sex education has failed to control the spiraling rate of teenage pregnancy and the spread of sexually transmitted diseases. The typical family is no longer—if it ever was—the intact two-parent model that often romantically lies behind the notion that sex education should be conducted at home. In a society saturated with sexual messages through advertising, magazines, television, and movies, we can hardly object that the discussion of family planning will be inappropriately provocative.

Tobacco and Alcohol. In the United States, 390,000 people die every year from the use of tobacco products, with costs of $22 billion in health care and $43 billion in lost productivity in 1985.[25] Former surgeon general Koop made a compelling case that tobacco contains compounds comparable in their addictive properties to illegal drugs like cocaine and opium.[26] According to Louis Sullivan, secretary of Health and Human Services in the Bush administration, "About 90 percent of smokers begin this addiction as children or adolescents. . . . The younger the age at which one begins to smoke, the more likely one is to become a long-term smoker and to develop smoking related diseases."[27] In 1987, over 26,000 persons died from alcohol-related chronic liver disease and cirrhosis. Alcohol is a factor in about 50 percent of traffic fatalities, and it also figures in spouse abuse and murder.[28]

Addictive substances like alcohol and tobacco not only kill people, but they also take away the ability to choose whether to use them. On both these grounds, then, crafting incentives for citizens to avoid addictive substances is well within the scope of the government's obligations as trustee. Although measures such as the ones suggested below will be attacked as paternalistic, an unwarranted interference with liberty, the charge is misdirected. The heart of the proposal is to preserve choice by decreasing the behaviors that lead to addiction. Any national health insurance scheme should include provisions for public education on the risks associated with alcohol and tobacco.

One measure that would be clearly justified in limiting the appeal of addictive substances would be to prohibit the advertisement of all alcoholic beverages and tobacco products in public places where viewing is de facto involuntary, including billboards. Similarly, such advertisements should be banned from public assets already owned by the state, such as the radio and television frequencies, as a condition of receiving a license.[29] Other measures might include the regulation of print advertising and increased taxation of tobacco products.[30] We should phase out all subsidies to tobacco farmers, even those subsidies now in force that allow cigarette companies to buy at below market prices from government-held surpluses.[31] An end to subsidies should be coupled with a program enabling farmers to develop alternative crops, of which many are possible.[32]

DUTIES BEYOND BORDERS

As we saw in chapter 5, one of the fundamental objectives of foreign policy on the fiduciary conception is to promote and/or protect the rights to political self-determination, minimal welfare, and bodily integrity of all people everywhere.[33] Since the people of one country have no legitimate common interest in how people of another country manage their traditions, other nations with legitimate democracies may operate within their own traditions and structure their own economies in any way they want, provided that the measures that they take do not undercut human rights or waste or destroy common natural resources. Actions of a state beyond its own borders can therefore be justified only because they are instrumental in protecting rights and our common heritage.

The trust conception also bounds our obligations, setting a limit to what justice beyond our borders requires. It does not prohibit wanted gifts beyond the minimum needed to satisfy basic rights and protect our common heritage, but it does show that they are not required. In a world of just and fiduciary regimes, all duties would stop at borders, except in cases of natural disasters. No nation is obliged to engage in free trade if doing so will curtail its productivity, damage the environment, impair the rights of its citizens, or erode democratically ratified traditions.

Looked at from this perspective, the world is in a mixed condition. During the Reagan/Bush era, the United States fell further and further behind in guaranteeing the subsistence rights of many of its citizens and also failed in many ways to protect the common heritage of mankind. Obviously, the situation is far worse in many other parts of the world. In China, for example, none of the three basic rights are secure. From Brazil to Indonesia, democracy is still very much in the institution-building stage, subsistence and other rights are insecure, and environmental degradation is substantial. In many countries, females are not accorded equal protection under the law and do not have the access to medical care that their male counterparts do. As a consequence, it is estimated that about 100 million girls and women who should be alive right now are dead, owing to female infanticide, lack of medical care, malnutrition, and brutality, a figure calculated by comparing female birthrates and the number of women actually in the population.[34]

In achieving a just international regime, the remedies for these rights violations are familiar ones: we are required to provide significant negative and positive international incentives for governments to respect the rights of their citizens. The case of South Africa is instructive and can be the cause of some optimism. A regime that failed with respect to all three basic human rights was changed, albeit over a long period, through coordinated international sanctions, until in the 1990s progress is being made without outside military intervention. Political enfranchisement will typically be a big step toward securing other rights. As Henry Shue points out, if rights are to be enjoyed *as* rights, political enfranchisement will always be necessary.[35] But it may not be sufficient.

Positive steps toward encouraging active trusteeship in other countries include foreign assistance programs that foster industrialization and the development of agriculture in ways that respect the environment. Here traditional large-scale projects need to be scrutinized with special care, to ensure that they really do help the poor meet subsistence needs and do not create environmental havoc. Because it concentrates on the vulnerability of persons, the fiduciary conception selects in favor of a "bottom-up" basic needs approach to foreign assistance, one that involves and strengthens people in meeting their own needs, rather than the traditional "trickle-down" framework, which often pays off mainly at the top end of the income distribution. We should also question the assumption that often goes with this view that more growth will lead to a more equal income distribution. Human well-being can at best be appropriately measured only indirectly by gains in gross domestic product (GDP) or gains in total GDP per capita.[36] Indeed, it is very likely that it is the time to replace, or at the very least substantially downplay, the GDP measure of progress. A very promising alternative school of thought concerned with enhancing human capabilities has been developing in and around the work of Martha Nussbaum and Amartya Sen.[37] It sees poverty as in part a result of ethical and conceptual failures in the way development is understood. Basically, it directs attention to the ability of persons to function along an array of capabilities and to their quality of life. (Nussbaum has argued that these concepts belong to the Aristotelian line of moral inquiry.) Of course, the best way to deliver aid may be to work with and give grants to international relief agencies such as the Red Cross, Planned Parenthood International, and OXFAM, rather than to develop additional or larger public bureaucracies.

It is crucially important not to assume that economic progress has to follow the wasteful and destructive path that it has in the United States.[38] Investment in energy-efficient technologies can leapfrog over many of the energy-intensive ways of increasing gross national product (GNP) and save money in the long run while helping stabilize global climate. This strategy *may* require greater initial costs, which will have to be borne by the industrialized nations. However, once the United States begins to get its own house in order with respect to energy use (a topic discussed in the next chapter), technological innovations that do not rely on fossil fuels, or that use them very efficiently, will almost surely become commonplace.[39] As these come on line, they can be transferred to the less developed world—in many cases with handsome profits to firms in the United States.

Within the trust conception of foreign policy, all countries must concern themselves as a matter of policy with their own birthrate and that of other countries because of the effects of high birthrates on subsistence rights and on the biosphere. Current high birthrates in the developing countries are having very negative effects on the ability of these nations to improve the economic well-being of their populations. As the UN secretary general stated at the 1992 Conference on Environment and Development, "Rapid population growth has acted as a brake on economic growth by diverting resources away from investment and hampering efforts to raise per capita income, education, and other ingredients of development."[40] For reasons that will be discussed more fully in the next chapter, there is growing evidence that the current mix of population, consumption patterns, and technology exceeds the long-run carrying capacity of the earth—imperiling the common heritage of mankind—and could lead to massive starvation if certain low-probability events, such as alterations in ocean currents, should occur. One key element in restoring ecological equilibrium is stabilizing and then reducing the human population.

Based on widely accepted long-term historical evidence, we can be sure that the political, educational, and economic enfranchisement of women will lead to a drop in fertility. As the world moves toward democracy and sustainable development, women can increase control over their own bodies if they have a full range of health care, birth control, and abortion options available. These changed roles for women will hasten the demographic transition to global replacement fertility or below—a transition that has already occurred in Europe and that could probably be achieved in the United States if we stopped suppressing the relevant information and technology.

On the fiduciary conception, rights serve to constrain both the traditions of a society and the operations of the market. But rights carry corresponding obligations and responsibilities. The right to reproductive information and control is easily distinguished from the right to have as many children as one cares to regardless of the quality of the care that one can give to those children. Obligations to control fertility extend well beyond considerations of family resources to consideration of the resources of the society (present and future) and of the planet, and wealthy and poor alike bear critical responsibility for their decisions about parenthood. No one's rights are violated by providing education about the social and ecological benefits of limiting family size. In the highly unlikely event that education, employment, and comprehensive health care for both mothers and children fail to bring the birthrate in the United States and elsewhere to a level below replacement, then tax incentives to control fertility could be reasonable next steps.[41]

NATIONAL DEFENSE BECOMES INTERNATIONAL PEACEKEEPING

The trustee model also puts national defense in another perspective, moving away from the competitive model that goes hand in hand with thinking in terms of competitive markets. It is, of course, the obligation of our government to preserve our property (in the broad sense of the term used by

Locke), but it is also its obligation—because government must discharge *our* duties—to preserve the lives of the citizens of other nations.

The fiduciary conception moves us in a direction different from that taken during the Reagan/Bush era because, in emphasizing the sanctity of human life, it helps us see risk management and uncertainty in the international sphere in a very different, more productive, and less expensive way. Rather than maintaining, at very high costs, the capability to defeat any potential adversary, or even any two adversaries at once, a view that looks at war as an ordinary way of doing business, we can manage the risk more intelligently and efficiently by cooperative regional and global security arrangements with other nations. As Kaufmann and Steinbruner put it,

> By accepting restraint, this posture imposes restraint on all potential sources of threat. Rather than treating threat contingencies as if they were determined by uncontrollable and undetectable processes of nature, a cooperative security arrangement uses political leverage to organize constraints on uncertainty. That is undeniably a more intelligent approach to uncertainty, and responsible security policy must attempt to develop it.

A foreign policy dedicated to protecting against any possible threat is indirectly unstable. For example, the current U.S. advantage in tactical air operations displayed in the 1991 Gulf War is unstable because "the core technology on which it is based is widely dispersed in international commercial markets, and it is those markets, rather than military programs, that are driving fundamental technical development."[42]

A world without war is not a utopian conception that only philosophers and dreamers can contemplate seriously. It is, ironically, what we already have within much of the developed world, and have had, with few exceptions, since 1945. As John Mueller notes,

> The long peace that has enfolded the developed world for so long has been the culminating result of a historic process in which the institution of war has gradually been rejected because of its perceived repulsiveness and futility. In the developed world few, if any, are able to discern either appeal or advantage in war any more; and they have come to value a goal—prosperity—that has long been regarded as incompatible with war. And, as the histories of countries like Holland, Sweden, Switzerland, and Denmark show, once a country drops out of the war system, it can manage for centuries to contain any enthusiasm for reentry.[43]

We have, Mueller convincingly argues, reached a consensus in the North Atlantic and beyond that war, like slavery and dueling, is a futile and immoral endeavor. A world without war does not require a new human nature any more than rejecting slavery did. It is not mainly the massive stockpiles of weapons that have not been used that has secured the peace but the commitment of the public to peace and prosperity that has, as Kenneth Boulding once remarked so succinctly, made war "obsolete."

The war against Iraq in 1991 might have been avoided altogether, or at least played out on a much smaller scale, had we pursued worldwide, or at the very least regional, disarmament. And an adequate energy policy (set out in the next chapter) would lessen American dependence on the Middle East and thus reduce one of our incentives for war in the first place. Widespread poverty and unemployment—factors that are at least aggravated by high rates of population growth—encourage the rise of dictatorial governments. If we can move to stabilize and then reduce the human population, we will make it more difficult for regimes of this sort to gain and hold political power. In addition, international sanctions against dictatorships as a general rule of world order will also help maintain or restore democratic governments.

To achieve the goal of "preserving all mankind" in the international arena, and to free up as much as possible of the hundreds of billions now being spent on weaponry, the international community should move toward outlawing war as a means of settling international disputes. Trusteeship is demanding but clear on this issue. While there is no way to stop all violence among human beings, there are ways to stop it in its institutional form. Here, although the Gulf War involved mixed motives, it provides a constructive model of an international force used to ensure compliance with at least some of the minimum standards of trusteeship. Cooperative security arrangements can be used to provide peacekeeping forces independently of or in conjunction with the United Nations. A very substantial additional benefit of stopping the spate of regional wars will be a reduction in the number of refugees in the world.[44] In addition, stopping the world arms trade will gradually diminish the destructiveness of civil wars when they occur, as current stockpiles will dwindle or cease to function.

On the fiduciary conception, the sale of arms either internationally or domestically is not just one transaction among many. In 1990, the world spent $21,726 million (in 1985 U.S. dollars) on the import of arms: the United States, the leading source, exported $8,738 million, the Soviet Union $6,373 million.[45] This trade is a signal of a willingness to violate the most fundamental of all moral obligations—the preservation of human life. In many regions of the world, nations are caught in an arms race with their neighbors. As one country or sect acquires new weapons, possible adversaries act or react accordingly, if they can, by increasing their own military capability. To break this downward spiral, we need to move toward a world order in which nations, and groups within nations, can be assured of protection against unprovoked attack. A first step in that direction is to move toward a world without an arms trade and with clear penalties for those who break this rule.

All nations engaged in the sale or purchase of arms or the sale or purchase of the means to construct arms—including the United States, the world's leading arms exporter—should be sanctioned by the most effective nonviolent means possible. Public pressure can be exerted simply by spotlighting the behavior of the noncomplying nation and contrasting it with the norm of international peace and a world without trade in the weapons of death. If action must be taken, trade sanctions can be threatened first, then applied if necessary. Foreign assistance and loans from entities like the World Bank can be made conditional on not trading in arms. In the (unlikely) event that these measures all fail, there should be an international capability, to be used under UN authority, to interdict arms or their components with sea, air, rail, and truck blockades, under the provisions of the UN Charter pertaining to international peace and security.[46]

A ban on the arms trade would leave the countries that have a substantial arms industry of their own, like the United States, France, China, and Brazil, in a comparative military advantage because they do not depend on importing weapons and their components. But the advantage will be diminished and more difficult to maintain because many of the economies of scale that attach to these industries result from the ability of these nations to engage in the international arms trade. An additional obstacle that should be created to undercut the usefulness of existing weapons stocks is an embargo on arms parts and components. Of course, some countries will continue to build arms despite these difficulties. Here the credibility of the United Nations or a default, possibly regional, peacekeeping force will be crucial by making it clear to any aggressor that the use of force against another nation will be met with force, followed, as in the Gulf War, by internationally enforced disarmament and the destruction of the aggressor's weapon-making capabilities.

The trust conception's international implications are especially hard on U.S. policy. Trusteeship calls on us to abandon the approach to foreign policy taken by all postwar administrations. The United States still actively engages in and promotes an international trade in arms. With the end of the cold war, we are faced with the opportunity to make amends. Stopping the arms trade and a shift to multilateral security arrangements must be seen not only as a chance to save money and invest at home but also as a fundamental duty of government.

Chapter 7

HOW TO STOP WASTING OUR CHILDREN'S HERITAGE

And Lord God took the man, and put him in the garden of Eden to dress and to keep it.

Genesis 2:15 (KJV)

For . . . labor being the unquestionable property of the laborer, no man but he can have a right to what that is once joined to, at least where there is enough and as good left in common for others.

JOHN LOCKE, *Second Treatise of Government*

The policies set out in the last chapter emerge from the government's direct duties to its beneficiaries. The trustee's duties of stewardship in the management of assets points to another set of issues on which the trust conception can cast new light. Governments as trustees have fundamental duties to preserve and enhance the value of assets, ranging from the cultural products of the past to the resources and an environment that will guarantee our future and that of our descendants. Indeed, the trustee model provides the theoretical underpinning—the conception of governmental legitimacy—necessary to ground the current and now nearly universal concern with sustainability.

By far the most important duties here pertain to the environment, and, on the fiduciary conception, concerns for the environment are central from the start.[1] Policies to preserve the environment are not newly discovered liberal causes arbitrarily or faddishly added to a long list of good things to do. The picture of government as a trustee of assets shows how environmental policies are organically linked to other progressive programs, from

111

election reform, to aid to the vulnerable, to a foreign policy dedicated to peace and the protection of human rights.

The material assets that government must preserve are of two broad types. One type includes assets on which all persons have a claim: the global atmosphere, the oceans, the productive farm- and forest land of the earth, and its genetic diversity. The second type includes those historical objects that belong to a group of particular individuals. The battlefield at Gettysburg belongs to Americans in a way that it does not belong to Canadians or the Japanese. Canterbury Cathedral is undeniably English. Roughly speaking, cultural assets belong to the people of the culture, whereas natural assets need to be managed (dressed) and preserved (kept) for the benefit of everyone—as Genesis 2:15 requires.

COMMON RESOURCES

The duty to preserve the common assets of the earth emerges fundamentally from the role of the trustee. But that role embodies a moral commitment that has roots in a number of traditions. Other religions than Judaism and Christianity hold that the earth is sacred because it is God's creation and that God intended not simply that we use it but also that we care for it.[2] To be a person—man, woman, or child—is to be a keeper of the earth. Moral equality requires that future generations have the same rights as the present generation to enjoy the earth's productivity and diversity. And many people believe, as Aldo Leopold would put it, that we have duties to the community of living things as such. On the matter of preservation of the biosphere and the creatures in it, there is a happy convergence between traditional theological beliefs about the sanctity of Creation, considerations of equality, and the perspective derived from ecology and evolutionary biology.

The present policies of the United States violate the duties of environmental stewardship in a number of ways. We harvest timber at a rate that exceeds the maximum sustainable yield of many of our national forests. We allow depletion of aquifers at rates that far exceed their recharge capacity. We sanction the waste of topsoil and encourage the destruction of prime farmland for easily relocated (or forgone) commercial and residential development. But by far our most pervasive and long-term abuses are of nonrenewable energy sources. Not only does their use deplete our supply, but their by-products disturb the global climate.

Stewardship of Climate. The well-known greenhouse effect is the warming of the lower reaches of the earth's atmosphere caused by the buildup of relatively large amounts of carbon dioxide and smaller amounts of other gases such as nitrous oxide and methane.[3] The likely results of greenhouse warming will be to change the average temperature near the earth's surface by as much as 1.5–4.5 degrees Celsius. In its 1988 report, the Environmental Protection Agency described the likely results of such a change:

> The findings collectively suggest a world that is different from the world that exists today. Global climate change will have significant implications for natural ecosystems; for when, where and how we farm; for the availability of water to drink and water to run our factories; for how we live in our cities; for the wetlands that spawn our fish; for the beaches we use for recreation; and for all levels of government and industry.
>
> For natural ecosystems (forests, wetlands, barrier islands, national parks) these changes may continue for decades once the process of change is set into motion. As a result, the landscape of North America will change in ways that cannot be fully predicted. The ultimate effects will last for centuries and will be irreversible. Strategies to reverse such impacts on natural ecosystems are not currently available.

Not only does the magnitude of the change matter, but so does the rate:

> The ability of society and nature to adapt to a global warming depends on the rate of climate change as well as the magnitude. If change is slow enough, nature can adapt through migration, and society can adjust through incremental investments in infrastructure improvements and the application of new technologies. A rapid climate change, however, may overwhelm the ability of systems to adapt.[4]

Most students of the greenhouse effect predict a substantial decline in average annual amounts of rainfall in the vastly productive midsection of the United States. While some of the resulting damage can be mitigated by such techniques as more efficient handling of remaining water resources and the breeding of drought-resistant crops, it is nevertheless likely that there will be a net decline in the productivity of American agriculture over the next century, although how great that decline will be remains unclear. There is no current evidence that American agriculture will be unable to produce enough food for our own population. Productivity declines will, however, affect U.S. exports and therefore the country's economic standing in the world. (Incidentally, the simplistic but often mentioned idea that productive agriculture will merely shift north into the Canadian tundra does not take into account the fact that topsoil there is thin and poor.) Increased ultraviolet radiation reaching the earth's surface caused by the thinning of the earth's ozone layer may further lower agricultural yields.

There is now a scientific consensus that global warming will contribute to a substantial rise in the sea level—as much as one and a half to three feet along portions of the East Coast of the United States in the next century.[5] Storm surge damage will therefore worsen, especially since storm frequency and intensity are both likely to increase. Flooding will require the construction of vast dikes or the loss of improved beachfront or coastline property and wildlife habitat. Poor low-lying countries such as Bangladesh will be especially devastated.

The broader community of plants and the other animals will be especially hard hit. Ecologically crucial wetlands lost along the coast in many places will not be able to re-form inland, much of the land having been developed for houses and shopping centers. Increases in water levels and temperatures over coral reefs will accelerate their rate of extinction and that of the many other animals and plants that depend on them. The rapid change in temperature zones will likely outpace the ability of many species to adapt or migrate, contributing to further extinctions around the globe. It is not expected that the temperature will rise very much near the equator. But there is a pattern of mutual dependence between plant and animal life there that, if upset, could devastate the region's biodiversity.[6]

Seen with the dangers of climate change in mind, the problem with the world's current stock of oil and other fossil fuels is not that it is too small but rather that it is too large. In the past, people have feared that an overall shortage of fossil fuels might curtail the development process. Now we must worry that fossil fuel availability feeds ecological imbalance. There is no reason to think that a shortage of fossil fuels will constrain environmental damage. Should the average consumption in China alone reach the world average, the destabilizing effects on the earth's biosphere would be catastrophic.

The fiduciary conception imposes an obligation on us to limit climate change because of our duties to conserve the range and quality of resources and because of our direct responsibilities to people who would be most affected.[7] As stewards of the natural world, we are also obliged to restrict climate change to a rate at which it will not be a factor in the extinction of species and the disruption of ecosystems. Stewards nurture and enhance their charge. They see themselves as a part of the natural order, which they therefore love and respect. Ultimately, as stewards, we must abandon the Cartesian subject-object dichotomy in thinking about our relations with nature.

Together these obligations amount to a de facto requirement to refrain from activities that materially disturb the natural process of climate change. Determining exactly the rate and the magnitude of the temperature change is beyond the scope of this book. We can be certain, however, that, to hold that change in the range of one degree per century, the world's nations must make a concerted effort to reduce the level of heat-trapping gases released toward that at which they are naturally removed from the atmosphere. The United States should seek to convene a convention to tighten the conditions of the climate treaty (so tragically weakened by the Bush administration in 1992) so as to reach such an equilibrium.[8]

Allocating responsibility for emissions reduction among countries is a problematic task, one complicated even further by the fact that, since population growth rates in part determine emission levels, climate stabilization therefore necessarily involves population control and reduction.[9] Because different countries experience different population growth rates, acceptable levels of emissions reductions must be carefully determined on a country-by-country basis to take account of individual circumstances. Countries unable to stabilize their populations, and therefore their emissions levels, might be given the option of increasing the efficiency of their energy use or of decreasing their energy consumption.

Population. Under the Reagan/Bush administrations, the United States was no longer willing to commit itself to stopping, or even slowing, world population growth. This inexcusable indifference to the effect that population growth has on a range of domestic and international problems has been defended by a variety of market theorists, for whom the question of the scale of human activity is not a serious consideration. In *The Ultimate Resource*, for instance, Julian Simon develops the simplistic thesis that there is no reason to worry about population growth because human inventiveness will always be able to solve seemingly insoluble problems.[10] On the basis of past evidence that human beings can solve problems faster than we create them, he argues that the growing number of problems created by population increase will without doubt be solved by the increased inventiveness that that growing population brings with it. Simon cites such factors as falling prices for natural resources, the use of less and less farmland to grow more and more food, and the alleged positive correlation between population and economic growth. The chief measure, then, becomes the relation between population growth and possibilities of consumption.

Of course, Simon ignores the fact that hundreds of millions of people are already malnourished. Also, the illiteracy of hundreds of millions wastes the "ultimate resources" that we already have, thus obviating any argument that we need more births to get more inventiveness. More important, he never considers the issue of whether the number of people on the earth exceeds the capacity of the earth to support them in the long run, not surprising for someone writing within neoclassical economics. In the two passages in Simon's book where "spaceship earth" is considered, no mention is made of the limits of the biosphere. The impending collision between population growth, technological advance, and the health of the biosphere shows that we are already overburdening the system.

Much of the confusion in the debate over whether and how to control population is generated by not distinguishing between the whole of the problem and a contributing part. It is often said that population is not the problem, that overconsumption is, or that population is not the problem because there still remain vast unpopulated areas around the globe. All that these arguments really do is point out what we already know: that population growth interacts with other factors in generating and aggravating problems. It is certainly true that the earth could support a larger population than it already does if, all else being equal, people consumed less.

The fiduciary conception imposes a double obligation on us to reverse the growth in human population. First, it is our duty to leave to future generations a world in which adequate resources are available, as are the means to dispose of waste products. Since the world's resources and its ability to absorb waste are limited, we must therefore "size" the world's population to them. Many countries in the world can no longer count on increased agricultural productivity.[11] Many countries have experienced a decline in the amount of grain available per person and have even sustained substantial damage to agricultural land. As population increases, the resource base per capita will shrink and eventually become inadequate—as it already has in many places. Conversely, maintenance of the resource base will escalate environmental damage. Eventually we will reach a point at which the population is so great, resources so few, and environmental damage so great that life on earth as we know it cannot be sustained. Climate change is but one indicator that we have already exceeded the planet's capacity to absorb waste. The more people, the more risk, at least in the ranges in which we are now operating.

Second, it is our duty to seek what Herman Daly has called the "biocentric optimum," at which other species and their habitats are preserved beyond the point necessary to avoid ecological collapse or cumulative decline, and beyond the point of maximum instrumental convenience, out of a recognition that other species have intrinsic value independent of their instrumental value to human beings. The biocentric optimal scale of the human niche would therefore be smaller than the anthropocentric optimum.[12]

The genetic diversity of the earth is a resource that belongs to all generations, past, present, and future, to "dress" and to "keep." To maintain the biocentric optimum we need to constrain population and consumption to levels low enough for other species to flourish. Given the high rate of species extinction already under way, it is clear that we have already exceeded these levels.[13]

The United States should target its own population for reduction. Leon Bouvier has suggested how to get to a population size of about 218 million people and, in what he calls his "hard scenario," has outlined a way in which we can attain this goal. To reach this goal, we should aim to lower the fertility rate to 1.5 live births per woman (a level above the present ones in the former West Germany and Austria) and to curtail net annual immigration at 300,000 (down from the current figure of roughly 800,000). Under this program, the population of the United States would peak at about 278 million in 2020 and then begin to decline, reaching about 218 million in the year 2080.[14] Such a program would not only reduce the many stresses on the environment in the United States but also make it easier and cheaper for the United States to do its share in restoring the global equilibrium among population, technology, and the environment. If these steps do not bring population growth in the United States (accounting for immigration) to a level below replacement, incentives should be put in place to limit family size, such as reducing or eliminating the child tax credit after two children.

As noted in chapter 6, however, few countries pursue aggressive family planning programs. Were the rights of women to control their own bodies respected and comprehensive health care made available to all mothers and children, the world would move a long way on the road toward stabilizing and ultimately reducing the human population. Toward this end, the United States should rejoin the UN Fund for Population Activities (UNFPA), which assists those countries that lack the necessary financial and technical resources to ensure that all women have access to family planning information and techniques.

Land. Locke's *Second Treatise* clearly justifies the private ownership of real property. But the thrust of his argument is that property should be in the hands of those who will use it well. In an age of unstable and often inadequate food supplies, Locke wanted agricultural land held by those who could and would make it productive. He abhorred the waste inherent in idle estates. The right to private property brought with it for Locke the obligation of stewardship: to use the land for the common good. Many Americans today, however, acknowledge only property rights and no corresponding fiduciary duties.

The public has a number of interests in private real property: its beauty, its role in the history of human and natural communities, the ecosystems of which private holdings are always a part, the quality of the air over it and of the water under it, and of course its productive capabilities. Current land use practices in the United States do not accord with those that would be followed under the trust conception of private property, contributing as they do to the waste of energy, the waste of farm- and forest land, and the destruction of ecosystems. A nation of mostly rural communities and vast areas of unspoiled countryside has been supplanted by the disorganized urban sprawl of single-family homes and shopping centers, committing us to overreliance on the automobile, building substantial energy requirements into our daily lives, and compounding our individual and national contribution to climate change.

Current land use practices in the United States also waste public financial resources. Decentralized settlement patterns require substantial and otherwise unnecessary capital investments in the infrastructure (roads, bridges, sewers, etc.), thus violating the trustee's obligations to care efficiently for the public's money. There are also substantial operating costs associated with providing school bus, fire, police, and ambulance service to a highly decentralized population. In some states, comprehensive plans for land use are not coordinated with zoning ordinances and therefore represent a great waste of time, effort, and money. Finally, farmland, which for all practical purposes cannot be replaced, is too often developed—and mostly unnecessarily since other land is usually equally suitable. The fragmentary character of private holdings and the nearly complete disregard of ecological principles in planning and zoning decisions assure that, if ecosystems are protected under our current policies, it will be by the happiest and most unlikely of coincidences.

To reduce such waste, the federal government should create very strong incentives for each state to concentrate development.[15] One possibility would be to tie any funding of projects by the Transportation Trust Fund to the development of a land use plan. John DeGrove has identified six useful guidelines for effective state land use plans.[16] First, county and municipality land use plans should meet stringent state guidelines. Second, plans to assure an adequate infrastructure—and to pay for that infrastructure—should be developed concomitantly with all land use plans. State aid for infrastructure costs can be withheld if county plans do not conform to state guidelines, thus making these first two policies mutually reinforcing. Third, state land use plans should emphasize compact urban growth patterns, thus reducing, and possibly even containing, urban sprawl, and urban design should be conceived on a more human scale. Fourth, government should help finance affordable housing. Most states that have growth management laws have implemented programs making affordable housing available to people with lower incomes and have found new sources of revenue to pay for those programs. Vermont, for example, has found a continuing source of funds in a real property transfer tax.[17] Fifth, land use plans should protect natural resource areas such as agricultural and forest lands. Finally, the plan should stimulate growth in areas with chronic unemployment or underemployment, although such traditional employment-generating projects as road construction that encourage and facilitate automobile use should be replaced by projects that contribute to a program of sustainable development and ecological restoration.

A promising model is for each state to divide all its land into three types of zones: (1) zones, typically near existing human settlements, in which a relatively high density of development, say, three to five family units to the acre is allowed; (2) resource management zones reserved for agriculture, forestry, aquifer recharge, etc.; and (3) ecologically sensitive zones designed to protect rare or endangered species, slopes too steep for farming or forestry, flood plains, and the like. Whenever possible, these ecologically sensitive zones should be structured in corridors, as opposed to islands, to facilitate the migration of species (particularly crucial in the event of continuing climate change). Such areas could be at least partially devoted to recreational uses, of course in ways consistent with the preservation of the natural communities within them. Ensuring that state laws reflect the stewardship conception requires planning from the point of view of "whole ecosystem management," which in many cases would involve planning for entire watersheds.[18] The Chesapeake Bay Agreement, a compact between the various jurisdictions in the Chesapeake watershed to limit runoff, is a first step in this direction and suggests that such arrangements are practical and at least somewhat effective. As a corollary to these state land use plans, the federal government should remove housing starts from the index of positive economic indicators. It is not, properly speaking, the number of new houses that are built that matters but rather the number of suitable units available relative to the number of households. A renovated house is as good as a new one from this perspective and does not involve the development of previously undeveloped land.

There is no reason whatsoever to think that such state land use plans would run afoul of the "takings" clause of the Fifth Amendment—the requirement that private property cannot be condemned and reclaimed by the state under the right of eminent domain without just compensation. This issue has been thoroughly tested in the courts. As John Humbach summarizes the current state of the law,

> Regulations limiting land to its existing uses meet the Supreme Court's test of economically viable use as long as the land retains some appreciable benefit in that existing use. The government's power to regulate or prohibit modifications to enable new *future* uses, without compensation, has not been questioned by the Court.
>
> It therefore is constitutionally permissible, according to the Supreme Court cases, to preserve the overall character of our national landbase and to prevent pockets of development from scattering across the countryside. Existing-use zoning can channel new construction projects to already developed areas, and the open lands in between can be retained as they are. The new land ethic of planning and stability need not founder on the property protections of our fundamental law.[19]

In 1992, the Supreme Court reaffirmed the traditional land use planning powers of the states.[20]

Under the fiduciary conception, the state has no obligation to compensate landowners who are restricted to using their land only in ways currently authorized since the fiduciary concept rejects the view that holds real property to be the owner's to use as she pleases.[21] In order to build strong political coalitions in support of such plans, it may, however, be necessary to devise temporary compensation systems. One model would be for the state government to tax some of the windfalls created for landowners within the designated growth areas to fund such a scheme. Alternatively, market mechanisms could be used by establishing or continuing a system of transferable development rights. Here landowners who were prohibited from development would receive credits for the loss of development rights and be able to sell "permits to build" in the designated growth areas.

Through its system of national parks, the U.S. government acts as a steward for ecosystems and for people. We hold such unique and beautiful areas in trust for ourselves and for all people as part of the common heritage of mankind. In recognition of this fiduciary obligation, the United States should classify those national parks with world significance as "World Heritage Sites," registering them as part of the UN system and publicizing them in that context much as Canada has with many of its national parks.

In order to preserve the earth's natural resource base and its biodiversity, conventions should be convened on international and regional bases— under the auspices of, say, the United Nations or regional bodies like the Organization of American States. Among the measures that such conventions should consider are, for example, the classification of soils on the basis of agricultural productivity under various climate regimes and the stipulation of appropriate land use and soil management practices, ones that will preserve, not destroy, prime agricultural and forest land. The 1971 Ramsar convention, which registers and then protects wetlands, should be expanded to include wetland areas worldwide.[22]

A national land use plan should reflect the responsibility of the United States under these international conventions—and do no less than they require. Nations that fail to exercise their responsibilities should be subject to the same gradually increasing sanctions as outlined for those who violate the human rights of their citizens because destroying the productivity and diversity of the biosphere is a violation of human rights and a violation of our obligations to the broader community of living things.

Ecological Restoration. A national land use program along the lines sketched above will do much to retard further waste of land, water, and air. However, by itself it will do little to repair damage that has already been done. The first step in a national program of restoration should be an inventory of damaged ecosystems and an assessment of what could be accomplished using existing techniques.[23] Obviously, reversing all human damage to the environment would be impossible and even undesirable. Priorities will have to be set. Federal work in the area should be coordinated with state land use plans so that our efforts are not counterproductive—for example, spending money to preserve ecosystems that are designated for development. Priority should be assigned to ecosystems that play important roles in the lives of endangered or threatened species.

Hunting. The debate over the constitutionality of laws restricting the possession of firearms naturally extends to a debate over the legitimacy of hunting itself. On the fiduciary model, hunting has two legitimate purposes. One is the maintenance of ecological order. In an ecosystem that remains relatively undisturbed by human activity, a balance exists among animals and plant populations that defines the carrying capacity of the system. Of course, carrying capacity changes over time, even without human intervention, and, for the most part, these changes are slow. But humans and human activity have been disrupting the natural balance at an ever increasing rate and in a number of ways: game managers remove predators to increase the number of game animals, acid rain changes the nature of soils, development depletes the water table, etc. Hunting is one of the mechanisms that we can use to restore an animal population to levels within the carrying capacity of an ecosystem. For example, in many parts of the United States, the deer population exceeds the carrying capacity of its range, leading to starvation and malnutrition among the deer and the destruction of young trees, crops, and other property. Hunting can be defended as a necessary evil in cases like this to balance the effects of human activity on ecosystems. In some areas, we can reduce our reliance on hunting by working to restore natural predators.

The other legitimate use of hunting, given the fiduciary conception, is in its role in the preservation of traditions. Among traditional peoples such as the Eskimo, hunting is carried on as a part of the historical heritage of the people and in some cases provides an important part of their food supply. Not only is it consistent with these practices, but it is required by them, that the animals hunted or fished continue to reproduce and flourish. International agreements concerning the hunting of whales, for example, recognize these rights of traditional peoples, while limiting the take to incidental percentages of the population.

Scale and Sustainability. The issues associated with climate change and the attendant problems of land use are subsets of a much larger set of problems concerning the scale of human activity as it relates to the biosphere of which, as noted in part I, neither the Right nor the centrist position takes account. By contrast, the key ecological notion of sustainability, which has been a crucial political and analytic tool of environmentalists, emerges naturally out of the idea of trusteeship and the obligation to preserve assets.

According to Herman Daly, "The main principle [of sustainability] is to limit the human scale (throughput) to a level which, if not optimal, is at least within carrying capacity and therefore sustainable." In order to limit the scale of present human activity, we must reduce our use of raw materials, thus avoiding disrupting the biosphere both when natural resources are extracted and when waste products are disposed of. The adoption of three subsidiary principles would allow us to accomplish this goal. (1) "Technological progress for sustainable development should be efficiency-increasing rather than throughput-increasing." That is, we should concentrate on those technologies that utilize raw materials most efficiently and produce fewer wastes. (2) With respect to renewable resources, "Harvesting rates should not exceed regeneration rates; and ... waste emissions should not exceed the renewable assimilative capacity of the environment." (3) "Nonrenewable resources should be exploited, but at a rate equal to the creation of renewable substitutes."[24]

PRESERVING OUR CULTURE

Beyond preserving the environment, which is part of the common heritage of humankind, government has a role in preserving the particular cultural heritage of the people or peoples of the nation. While the market model emphasizes that aspect of human nature concerned with consumption, the fiduciary conception takes a broader, more inclusive view. We are creatures of culture, of history, who understand ourselves and the world around us through symbols. Our language—and therefore our view of the world and our place in it—draws on literature and the arts and on the histories of particular places.

Many sites in the United States—from Plymouth Rock and Jamestown to the battlefields at Little Big Horn and Gettysburg, from drive-in movie theaters to state capitol buildings, from log cabins to plantation homes—are of special significance to us. And many Americans find different meanings in these sites. We preserve them, not because we all agree on what they mean or that they are even meaningful, but because the process of debate, interpretation, and argument makes it possible to see that we have a common history, that our understandings and misunderstandings of each other have deep roots, and that, when we understand these roots, we are on the way to Locke's central virtue: tolerance.

Much of the land and many of the buildings and artifacts that make up our common history are in private hands and can be legally destroyed or altered. For example, much of the area surrounding the historic battlefield at Antietam is threatened by commercial and residential development. To retain the integrity of our parks and protect our historic landmarks, Congress should pass the National Heritage Conservation Act, which requires the secretary of the interior to work with state governments and private citizens to avert the degradation and destruction of parks and historic sites and to protect and preserve landmark buildings.[25]

The government should also pursue policies that nurture and promote public participation in the humanities and the arts. Existing programs such as the National Endowment for the Humanities and the National Endowment for the Arts represent important forces and should be encouraged as central to our self-understanding as a nation of extremely diverse people.

DEFENDING "ROBUST" STEWARDSHIP

Those within the market schools that I discussed in part I will argue that I have misconstrued the notion of stewardship. Many concede that we have an obligation to leave the future at least as well off as we are, but then argue that this duty can be discharged simply by leaving our descendants with at least as much savings and other forms of capital as we have. According to this view, we have no way of knowing what people in the future are going to want in particular, so we might just as well leave them capital and let them decide for themselves how to use it.

This view is much too simple. Although there are good reasons for saving money for our descendants to use, there is no good reason to think that this is all we must do. You cannot eat or drink money. There is no plausible account of our obligations to future generations that justifies imperiling the food and water supply or allows the destruction of the earth's agricultural lands, forests, and wetlands. The argument that enough of these productive resources will be conserved by the market—their price rising as they become more scarce—ignores the irreversibility of many actions. Once it is filled and paved over, a wetland can be restored only with extreme difficulty—at best. Once a species is destroyed, it cannot be regenerated—ever. The simple possession of capital will not be enough to let a future generation determine that it does in fact value and therefore wish to preserve a species once it has gone extinct. If the market school argues that we have to adjust prices to reflect the true cost of these kinds of losses, we are back to the problems of discounting: losses that occur more than a few years hence will be assigned a trivial value. And, if one concedes that discounting is inappropriate, one has in fact begun to draw on the fiduciary conception, which I have argued grounds and gives content to the centrist position.[26]

The economists' account of intergenerational obligations ignores the role of culture and symbol in human life altogether and hence cannot ground the obligation to preserve culture—the means by which we interpret the world and our place in it. They ignore the importance of community, of people in places. If we are serious about our moral and religious life, then we have to preserve the communities and places that sustain us and give our lives much of the meaning that they have. The burning of the library at Alexandria, which destroyed irreplaceable manuscripts from ancient Greece and Egypt, was not only a waste of parchment.

Another attempted refutation of the fiduciary model might claim that any interference with a perfectly functioning market will harm the poor. The bitter and tragic irony of this claim should be completely apparent. Having embraced a framework that has *nothing* systematic to say about the distribution of goods essential for life and self-respect, to claim to be concerned with the poor is a charade, a desperate attempt to save the framework, not the poor. Ironically, it is a defense often mounted by people who insist that moral language other than their own is meaningless.

PUTTING TRADE IN PERSPECTIVE

The fiduciary account narrows and helps specify the domain in which free trade is appropriate. Governments violate their fiduciary obligations when they engage in trade practices that undercut the subsistence rights of their own citizens. Similarly, they neglect their duties when they engage in trade practices that undermine the long-term well-being of their resource base or undercut biodiversity.[27] Practices such as exporting timber at a rate that outstrips the speed with which forests can be replenished are incompatible with maintaining the resource base. Programs that encourage and subsidize reforestation are not illegitimate interferences with the marketplace, as the General Agreement on Tariffs and Trade suggests; they are, rather, among the central duties of the trustee.

The same can be said concerning human traditions. If they wish to do so, the Swiss, for example, are perfectly entitled to preserve their historic landscapes through subsidizing their dairy farmers or through erecting trade barriers against foreign imports. Of course, since rights claims are prior to those based on traditions, *if* such practices interfere with the ability of others to maintain their subsistence rights, then protectionist practices are illegitimate, unless other steps to secure those rights are taken. Free trade is to be judged on instrumental grounds. It is not a good in itself.

Indeed, trade negotiations are one of the incentives that nations can use to get other nations to discharge their obligations to their citizens and the biosphere.[28]

All movement toward free trade agreements should be halted until those agreements can be made part of a comprehensive set of treaties concerning the government of the global commons.[29] They should include international agreements that protect the world's forests, wetlands, and biodiversity. In addition to an international convention on climate, conventions should be convened to address the problems of population growth, the sharing of advanced technology, poverty, and pollution. As part of a comprehensive package of agreements to protect ourselves and our common heritage, nations should be free to enter into free trade agreements if they choose and if those agreements are not harmful in other ways, but there is no obligation to do so.

Chapter 8

PAYING FOR A SUSTAINABLE, RESPONSIBLE SOCIETY

Raising children, preserving nature, cherishing art, and practicing the virtues of civil life are all costs—the costs of being the people we are. Why do we pay these costs? We can answer only that these costs are benefits; these actions justify themselves; these virtues are their own reward.

MARK SAGOFF, "Zuckerman's Dilemma"

The state is a product of society, an expression of it, an image of it. It is a structure that a society creates for itself as an instrument of its own self-realization.

VACLAV HAVEL, 1990

The rich should regard themselves as trustees for the whole of society rather than as owners of the wealth they might possess.

MAHATMA GANDHI, 1934

Of course government programs must be paid for, and the government raises money through taxation. On the trust conception, taxes are an appropriate instrument by which government achieves its legitimate purposes, not, as the market theorists would have it, a necessary evil that should interfere as little as possible with the operation of the marketplace. When we understand that the theory of market failures cannot provide an adequate foundation for state legitimacy, we are able to see the possibilities of taxation in a new and positive light. Of course, taxes still take something from us, but what they can give us in return—in addition to the direct and tangible benefits we receive—is a well-ordered and just society and a stable world that respects human rights and the health of the biosphere, matters well worth investing in as citizens of a responsible society.

LIFE AND TAXES

Taxes provide government with the funds to discharge its four classes of duties under the trust model: promoting efficient markets; keeping markets, needs, merit goods, and fiduciary goods in proper balance; protecting human rights; and ensuring the productivity and diversity of the biosphere. Therefore, how governments raise money and how they spend it reveal the structure of public morality, what the citizens value as a society. There are many ways in which taxation can be used to advance the moral concerns of trusteeship and direct the activities of the market toward the public good. (Of course, using taxes to influence the market is something government already does, and did more of before the distortions of the market model began to take hold of public policy.)

Taxes may, for example, be used to control the price of such commodities as gasoline the excessive consumption of which threatens the biosphere or to provide for nonrival public goods such as parks and museums. Tax deductions and tax credits can act as incentives for owners of historic properties to preserve them for future generations. Tax deductions can support education by encouraging gifts to colleges and universities, provide incentives for people to give to the poor, or stimulate the interest of developers in constructing housing for low-income households. Tax incentives can even be used to encourage agricultural practices based on the notion of a sustainable yield.

This is not to say that direct regulation is not also a legitimate exercise of state power under the fiduciary conception. Of course it is. But the trustee can use a variety of instruments in discharging the government's fiduciary responsibilities, in many cases making use of institutions other than the state. Achieving the legitimate purposes of the state through tax incentives and credits joins the efforts of private entities like Planned Parenthood, the Red Cross, and the Nature Conservancy (which ought to be encouraged by government policy) as means of accomplishing what needs doing. Thus, the fiduciary conception can join the Right and the Marxist Left in championing the merits of a streamlined state. The benefits of privatization and other market mechanisms such as vouchers, often advocated by the Right, can easily be made use of by the trustee.

The fiduciary conception of the state provides a way of setting public taxing and spending priorities, although not with a single decision rule, as cost/benefit analysis purports to do. Since the duties of the trustee are rank ordered, we have a way of determining which priorities are the most important. In the balance of this chapter, I set out some cost estimates for the illustrative fiduciary program that has been discussed in the previous two chapters. Those opposed to a trust conception of government will argue that we simply cannot afford to fund expensive programs, or that we cannot afford to raise taxes, or that the public will not stand for higher taxes. The truth is that we cannot afford *not* to do these things. Continuing the status quo will ensure the destruction of much of the biosphere and increase injustice and instability at home and around the world.

A more just and stable society and world can be achieved at little or no additional cost. The figures that I use have been supplied by others, and in my documentation can be found references to the methodologies used in order to arrive at those figures. The numbers presented below are not hard and fast, simply illustrative of the order of magnitude of the costs.

A FIDUCIARY BUDGET

If we sum up the expenditure and revenue needs of the fiduciary conception, we get the very rough approximation that appears in table 1. The numbers cited are *increases* or *decreases* with respect to expenditures at the time the estimate was made. I have drawn on a number of sources cited in the text. They do not all make estimates for the same year, and the estimates are arrived at by means of different methodologies. Nevertheless, the table gives a useful "order of magnitude" estimate of the cost of a return to a responsible society. One of the most remarkable things that the table reveals is how inexpensive discharging some of these fiduciary responsibilities would be.

Of course, there will most likely be some interactive effects of these budget changes. Increased foreign assistance may cause greater demand for American products, thus yielding more jobs and tax revenues. Reducing the number of unwanted births will reduce welfare rolls and free many people to work. If we gave $1,000 to everyone with a child in the home, we would reduce the number of families living in poverty and thus cut the number eligible for housing assistance. Cleaning up toxic wastes will likely overlap with ecological restoration. I have not included savings so generated. Nor have I included costs of other things worth doing under this

TABLE I. A Fiduciary Budget

A. Expenditures	% change in GNP	B. Sources of Funds	% change in GNP
Duties of merit		*Protecting the vulnerable*	
Public financing of		Defense spending cuts	1.75
congressional campaigns	.004	International security	
Duties to the vulnerable		assistance cuts	.01
Agenda for children	.81	*Enhancing choice*	
National health insurance	.97	Alcohol and tobacco taxes	.01
National housing assistance		*Stewardship taxes*	
program	.30	Carbon tax	.9
Purchase of firearms	.05	Gasoline tax	.9
Foreign development		Severance taxes	.2
assistance	.50	*Duties of the rich*	
Enhancing choice		Raise marginal tax rates for	
International family		individuals	.37
planning	.04	Estate taxes	.05
Duties of stewardship		*Total*	4.19
National Heritage			
Conservation Act	.02		
Clean up toxic waste sites	.21		
Sustainable agriculture	.02		
Climate stewardship	.88		
Ecological restoration:			
Species recovery	.009		
Restoration inventory/			
demonstration	.009		
Total	3.82		

Note: GNP for 1991 was $5,685.8 billion.

model. Under the market regime, nurturing of the arts has languished, and minds are wasted because people cannot afford the costs of higher education. If we continue to experience severe economic dislocations, a workers' retraining superfund may be necessary. Carbon taxes may slightly reduce GNP.

In addition to the requirement that we preserve certain definite things, such as biological diversity, by requiring that the assets of the trust be conserved, and if possible enhanced, for future beneficiaries, the fiduciary conception also gives us a way to think about the size of the overall saving

Restoring the Public Trust

rate. This duty is violated if we leave a large burden of debt or a degraded resource base for our descendants. This is obviously not a requirement that we avoid using the earth or the fuels and minerals in its crust. It is, however, a requirement that each generation leave its successors at least the same net capability to benefit from the resources, or from substitutes, as it itself enjoys. Hence, the government may have an obligation to stimulate savings, and this rate will have to be added to the presentation in table 1 since it will allocate part of GNP away from present consumption patterns.

HOW TO GET TRUSTEES WE CAN TRUST

As I have suggested, we cannot trust the impartiality of our current leaders because public office is both de facto and de jure for sale, for reasons set out in chapter 6. The Congressional Budget Office (CBO) has estimated the costs of election reform as set out in proposed House legislation.[1] Were each candidate for a seat in the House to receive $200,000 to cover campaign expenses, the maximum that would be required from federal coffers would be an average of $88 million each year. The necessary funds would come in part from general revenues and in part from fines levied against those who do not comply with campaign finance laws. To help reduce the advantage to incumbents, limited lower-cost mailing could be made available to nonincumbents at an average cost of $25 million a year. Thus, the average annual cost of House elections would be about $113 million. This is the highest-cost scenario since the figures given represent maximum utilization of federal funding opportunities. A voluntary system could cost considerably less, depending on the rate of participation (some candidates with access to other resources might not be willing to participate owing to overall spending limits).

The CBO has also estimated the costs of a similar bill in the Senate.[2] Under the provisions of this bill, the reduced postal charges to candidates for Senate seats would be about $8.5 million annually. Payments from a campaign fund established by the bill would be about $29 million annually if every state's Senate election had two eligible candidates. Thus, total costs would be about $37.5 million annually. Obviously, if the spending limits are set higher, the costs will be higher. Under the assumptions used for the CBO estimates that I have cited, the total average cost would be about $175 million a year. This is a low price indeed for trustees we can trust.

The fiduciary conception of the state also helps us settle a controversy over the use of the broadcast media in the context of elections. It provides a legitimate philosophical foundation for the fairness doctrine. As Owen Fiss puts it,

> The fairness doctrine—a body of government regulations that has evolved through agency action, case law, and congressional regulation—consists first of a requirement that broadcasters cover issues of great public importance. The second and more frequently litigated part of the doctrine requires that the coverage of such public issues be balanced.[3]

Under the ill-considered program of the Right, the fairness doctrine has been abolished by the Federal Communications Commission, an action that has been upheld by the courts. The main ground for rejecting the doctrine was that it interfered with journalists' rights of free speech.[4]

The trust conception of government legitimacy opts in favor of a return to the fairness doctrine on two distinct grounds. First, it makes it clear that the broadcast part of the airwaves is part of the common heritage of humankind. On Locke's conception, airwaves can be considered real property and may therefore be appropriated. They may be converted into private property, but only on the condition that as such they serve the public good. Indeed, the regulatory model underlying much of broadcast law is called the *public-trustee concept.*[5] Second, once we see the role of the state as defining an appropriate but limited role for the market and keeping it distinct from merit goods, we can readily understand why the institutions on which democratic debate rests must be open to all who are above some rather easy to satisfy threshold of credibility as candidates. Without something like the fairness doctrine, few but the rich have access to the means of political persuasion, and therefore the market illegitimately dominates the terms and content of political discourse. On the fiduciary conception, as Fiss puts it, "We turn to the state because it is the most public of all our institutions and because only it has the power to resist the pressures of the market and thus to enlarge and invigorate our politics."[6] Thus, the fiduciary conception is not only compatible with but also demonstrates the legitimacy of requiring that candidates be given free airtime so that political choices can be based on full and open debate.

PROTECTING THE VULNERABLE

Children. The cost of implementing the policies for children outlined in chapter 6 total between $44 and $48 billion a year. Of this, $40 billion goes for the child tax credit, between $1 and $4 billion for Head Start, and about

$1 billion for the WIC program. (I follow the estimates of the National Commission on Children here, with the exception of those for health insurance, which I discuss separately below.)

National Health Insurance. Henry Aaron estimates that providing acute care under his "universal-access single-payer health plan" would cost $40 billion a year, while long-term care would add about $25 billion (in 1991 dollars). Thus, the total increased cost to the federal government would be about $65 billion for the Aaron plan.[7]

The Pepper Commission's recommendation that the government provide health insurance to everyone would raise the costs to the public sector by $24 billion a year (in 1990 dollars). The costs of the commission's recommendation that long-term care be expanded are about $19 billion a year (in 1990 dollars).[8] Thus, the total would be about $43 billion a year in new federal expenditures—a number that approximates the federal government's estimate of the productivity losses associated with smoking. In table 1 I use a rough average of these and Aaron's numbers to estimate the costs of discharging this fundamental obligation of the trustee.

Housing. The CBO estimates that a voucher system to house all participating persons whose incomes are less than 50 percent of the median income of their area, with the household paying 30 percent of adjusted income, would cost $11.1 billion in 1990.[9] This does not include a figure for the homeless whom we see on our streets. If we assume that this number is somewhere between 400,000 and 700,000 and take the average of these figures, we get 550,000. Participation in a program would almost certainly not exceed 500,000, and, at $6,000 per person per year, this would cost another $3 billion at the most.[10] Hence, the cost of a national housing assistance program would be in the range of $14–$15 billion.

Firearms. According to the Bureau of Alcohol, Tobacco, and Firearms, there are about 201,837,000 guns in private hands in the United States. Of these, about 66,000,000 are handguns, 73,000,000 rifles, and 62,000,000 shotguns.[11] In chapter 6, I proposed that the government purchase all handguns and all fully or semiautomatic rifles and shotguns not owned by the military or law enforcement agencies. Let us now explore the implications of such a policy, which is like one recently implemented in the City of St. Louis.

If we estimate that there are 17,000,000 automatic rifles and the same number of automatic shotguns—an estimate that is probably too high—the federal government would need to buy 100,000,000 guns. If the government were to start paying $200 per gun in the first year of the program, and if 50 percent of the guns were turned in that year, the program would cost $5 billion. If in each successive year the amount paid per gun declined by 20 percent, and if 10,000,000 guns were purchased each year, the results would be as follows: year 2, $1,600,000,000; year 3, $1,200,000,000; year 4, $800,000,000; and year 5, $400,000,000. The total cost of the program would be $14 billion, or an average of $2.8 billion a year over the five-year period. The program would, of course, result in reduced costs in other areas, many of which had previously been borne by the public—for example, costs associated with treating those wounded by guns or supporting children who had lost a parent. Most important, a new climate of civility would begin to take shape.

Securing the Peace. Kaufmann and Steinbruner's reorientation of defense set out in chapter 6 leads to a defense budget based on the assumptions of a cooperative security arrangement that requires annual expenditures of about $147 billion (in 1992 dollars) in 2001 and that accomplishes an annual saving of about $97 billion (in 1992 dollars) in 2001 when compared with a Bush administration plan.[12] The cumulative resulting savings would total $424 billion between 1992 and 2001 (in 1992 dollars).

As a stable and verifiable international order is established, we should be able to realize even greater cost savings, by eliminating foreign military financing and other forms of security assistance altogether. Since these expenditures do not currently appear as part of the Department of Defense budget, they would result in an additional annual saving of just short of $8 billion.[13]

Also, as verifiable evidence is obtained that other nations have abandoned their nuclear forces, further reductions in our nuclear arsenal could be safely affected, thereby cutting the defense budget even more. These possible savings of as much as half Kaufmann and Steinbruner's projections would leave us with expenditures of $73 billion (in 1992 dollars) in 2001, a saving of more than $170 billion over Bush administration projections. Simply halving all of Kaufmann and Steinbruner's figures might not be the best approach to take. Even were we to do so, however, we would be left with 1,500 intercontinental warheads, three to four army divisions, one to two marine air wings, three carrier battle groups, twenty amphibious ships, and hundreds of planes and dozens of ships for air- and sealift capability. Cutting these figures in half yet again would yield additional savings of over $200 billion a year.

Foreign Development. To give an example of the budget implications of fulfilling our duties to help the world's poor and to protect the environment in the less developed countries, we can use the UN figure of o.7 percent of GNP as a target for official development assistance. According to the Development Assistance Committee of the Organization for Economic Cooperation and Development (OECD), the United States contributed o.21 percent of its GNP to foreign development in 1990, down from an average of o.23 percent over the years 1977–81. Denmark, the Netherlands, Norway, and Sweden already exceed the UN target of o.7 percent. A majority of nations sitting on the Development Assistance Committee accept that the UN goal is appropriate.[14] In order to comply with these guidelines, the United States would have to contribute about $38 billion annually (a figure based on 1990 GNP). However one calculates appropriate levels of spending, much more needs to be done to define and implement a strategy of sustainability from foreign assistance as well as in domestic policy.[15]

ENHANCING CHOICE

Stabilizing World Population. The dollar cost of addressing population growth is astonishingly small, and great progress could be made simply by making contraceptives widely available. With increased overall development assistance, population activities can be included in a comprehensive program to increase literacy and employment and improve health care in the Third and Fourth Worlds. The UN Population Fund estimates that, "if all women who said they wanted no more children were able to stop childbearing, the number of births would be reduced by 27 percent in Africa, 33 percent in Asia, and 35 percent in Latin America."[16] To be truly effective, family planning has to be placed in the context of a broad program providing health care to mothers and children. On the fiduciary conception, all governments have a responsibility to increase literacy rates as well as the rate of participation in democratic processes among both women and men.

To extend family planning services to the 92 million couples in the world who do not desire another pregnancy would cost about $2 billion more a year. A comprehensive program aimed at reaching 500 million people, reducing infant mortality to fifty per thousand live births, reducing teenage pregnancies and maternal mortality by 50 percent, providing family planning to 60 percent of all newlyweds, integrating family life education into the curriculum, and increasing women's education and literacy would require an increase in assistance from the current $500 million to $5 billion.

An even more aggressive and comprehensive program would cost $12–$20 billion by the year 2000.[17]

The Population Crisis Committee estimates that we could hold maximum human population size to 9–10 billion, slightly less than twice the current population, by supplying contraceptive services to 75 percent of the couples in (the mainly developing) countries that now have an average family size of more than two children.[18] According to the committee, this would require worldwide expenditures of $10.5 billion: the breakdown proposed by the committee is $1 billion from consumers in the countries in question, $4 billion from developing country governments, $1 billion from the international development banks, $500 million from private philanthropy, and $4 billion from the governments of the industrialized countries. If the developed countries doubled their average development assistance and then allocated 4 percent of this to population and family planning, the $4 billion goal would be achieved. Thus, family planning would occur in a context of overall economic development. Developed countries already spend $4 billion on their military establishments every two days. If the United States met the UN goal for international aid discussed above, the amount for population and family planning would be about $2 billion, approximately four times the current level. Average annual contributions by Americans to official development assistance would be about $175 per capita, $8.00 of which would go toward activities meant to stabilize population.

Alcohol and Tobacco. In general, taxes on alcohol and tobacco are lower in terms of constant dollars than they were forty years ago, with the exception of table wine. On the basis of Congressional Budget Office projections, increasing the tax on a pack of cigarettes from the $0.24 effective 1 January 1993 to $0.32 would raise $1.5 billion annually by 1996. Revenues from this source should decline gradually over time as programs to retard and prevent the addiction of the young have time to work.

Increasing the tax on beer, wine, and distilled liquor to $0.25 per ounce of ethyl alcohol would raise about $4.6 billion. This would increase the tax on a 750 milliliter bottle of distilled spirits from about $2.14 to $2.54, the tax on a six-pack of beer from $0.33 to $0.81, and the tax on a 750 milliliter bottle of wine from $0.21 to $0.70. These taxes should be indexed to inflation to keep the effective rate of the tax from falling and to avoid the need for abrupt increases in the future. By 1996, the increased tax on alcohol would raise $4.6 billion annually.[19]

PAYING FOR STEWARDSHIP

National Land Use Plan. No additional federal revenues would be required for this measure. Incentives for state compliance can be derived from withholding Transportation Trust Fund monies from states without suitable plans. States should save large amounts in infrastructure and service provision costs as the benefits of more clustered development take hold, thus reducing the pressure on state budgets.

National Heritage Conservation Act. The proposed annual budget for the National Heritage Conservation Act is $25 million. This is inadequate since it would allow the purchase of only twenty-five million-dollar properties annually. I propose increasing the budget to $1 billion and allowing some funds to flow to private land and historic trusts, which typically work to secure easements from private landowners on ecologically sensitive areas, on productive farm- and forest land, and on sites and buildings of historic importance. These organizations could work hand in hand with state governments in protecting land, and in some cases buildings, identified as of special significance. Priorities for preservation could be generated on the basis of ecological sensitivity, productivity (of farm- or forest land), and historic importance.

Toxic Waste Cleanup. The Waste Management Research and Education Institute of the University of Tennessee at Knoxville has undertaken a study of the total costs of cleaning up the nation's hazardous waste sites. Under the institute's auspices, Milton Russell, William Colglazier, and Mary English have developed three cost options that do not "differ in terms of the residual health and environmental risks to which persons and natural systems may plausibly be exposed now or in the future."[20] Russell et al. estimate a mean cost of $750 billion over a thirty-year period, or $25 billion a year. Of these costs, about $12 billion annually would accrue to the federal government in addition to what is being spent now on toxic waste cleanup. The bulk of this, $8 billion a year, would be for cleanup of nuclear waste at Department of Energy sites. As weapons production slows, or better stops, waste production will decline as well.

Ecological Restoration. The Office of the Inspector General has estimated that to assist the recovery of all species now officially listed as endangered or expected to be listed would cost $4.6 billion over a ten-year period, or about $500 million a year.[21] Proper land use planning would protect ecologically sensitive areas. Eventually, the cost of protecting endangered species should gradually decrease as the need to do so disappears. Estimates of the cost of restoring damaged ecosystems have not yet been developed, but I would suggest an appropriation of $500 million a year to develop the inventory discussed in chapter 7 and of another $500 million to begin some demonstration projects. In the event that we need to stimulate the economy to create employment, these projects should be prime candidates for government-initiated jobs.

Agriculture. Because agriculture affects human and ecological health so greatly, its redirection is a vital aspect of the fiduciary program. Much more work needs to be done on defining alternative and sustainable agriculture and in providing demonstrations of its feasibility. I propose that $1 billion be spent on such preliminary work, a figure up from the approximately $94 million being spent annually in the early 1990s.[22] Many new practices can be implemented by farmers without any financial assistance at all or simply by redesigning existing incentive programs.

Energy. Because of the risks to our descendants and to the stability of ecosystems associated with climate change, the trust conception requires that we stabilize the climate. Various plans have been put forward that would reduce the amount of heat-trapping gases released into the atmosphere—especially carbon dioxide—through market incentives. For example, a tax on carbon in various fuels would create incentives to shift to fuels that contain comparatively less carbon, or to sources such as solar and wind that emit no carbon, or to more efficient fossil fuel technologies. Obviously, the higher the tax, the stronger the incentives. There are a variety of ways to cushion the burden of these taxes on the poor, from direct rebates through the tax system to exempting certain portions of utility bills from taxation. Revenues generated by the carbon tax (say, $50 billion) should be "recycled" to create direct incentives to energy consumers to engage in practices that reduce the emissions of heat-trapping gases.

Florentin Krause has set out a well-considered strategy to curb and modify our energy consumption.[23] Federal regulations should be developed that eliminate the most inefficient appliances, lightbulbs, and vehicles from the marketplace altogether. In addition, fiscal and regulatory changes should be enacted that allow established energy-supply industries to engage in special profit-making opportunities, prompting demand-side investments among consumers and thus reducing emissions of heat-trapping gases. Even if the government fails to implement recycling programs, the work of these programs could be accomplished by a more generalized investment tax credit, paid for by the revenues from a climate stewardship tax. This investment tax credit, coupled with higher prices for carbon-intensive fuels, would provide generalized incentives for adopting energy-efficient and less polluting technologies.

To reach the target of a 20 percent reduction of greenhouse gas emissions (as compared to 1985) between now and the year 2015 (set out in note 8 of chapter 7) would require levying a carbon tax of about $60.00 a ton, phased in between now and the year 2005. This tax would generate about $50 billion a year.[24] In addition to this "climate stewardship" tax, there should be an increase in the gasoline tax of $0.50 a gallon, which would augment general revenues by about $50 billion. These two taxes should be phased in over a three- to five-year period to allow consumers time to adjust their behavior and the processes of government-spurred innovation and substitution to take effect. Coupled with national land use planning, the gasoline tax will create further incentives to stop wasteful, decentralized land use patterns. It is important to note that fuel prices would still be substantially *below* those charged today in the European Community.

Severance and Disposal Taxes. To attain sustainability, measures must be implemented to reduce throughput in areas beyond the energy sector. Severance taxes should be imposed on minerals, forest products, and the like along with taxes on disposal of such things as mine tailings, newspaper, and effluents from industrial processes.[25] These are shown for illustrative purposes in table 1 as .2 percent of GNP. In general, it may be better to rely on consumption taxes than on income taxes.

DUTIES OF THE RICH

While the fiduciary conception clearly allows inequalities in wealth, even great inequalities, it also requires that this wealth be used for the public good. The vulnerability model grounds the duties of the rich by showing that there is a direct relation between power and responsibility. Accordingly, the more wealth a person has, the greater the obligation. In the past, one of the chief ways of harnessing the income of the wealthy for the common good has been through progressive taxes, which take higher percentages of income as income rises. One of the primary arguments that conservatives use against progressive taxation is that it undercuts work incentives. They argue that, as people can retain less of their income per hour worked, they will work less, substituting leisure for work. Interestingly, this argument—that progressive taxes undercut work incentives and thus harm everyone through decreased economic activity, employment, inventiveness, and the like—already concedes that the issue should be examined in terms of its effect on the public interest.

There is, therefore, nothing wrong with the normative framework in which the issue is placed. The problem with the argument is that its empirical premise is not true. Lower marginal tax rates seem to have virtually no effect on work incentives. This has been amply demonstrated by C. V. Brown.[26] While lower tax rates are expected to create incentives to work harder, this effect is canceled out by what can be called the *wealth effect*. At lower marginal tax rates, people retain more income for less work. What such people actually do is to devote more time to leisure. The argument of the Right about the incentive effects of lower marginal tax rates also fails to take into account the fact that many people do not have the opportunity to work more even if they want to.[27] Once we make the commonsense observation that many people work because they like to, pay being incidental, the supposed anomaly, that progressive taxes do not discourage work, becomes even less difficult to explain.

The National Commission on Children estimated that increasing the top marginal tax rate from 31 to 50 percent for joint returns with taxable income over $300,000 (with proportional changes for other categories of taxpayers) would generate about $21 billion in 1993. Changing the exemption for estate taxes from $600,000 to $300,000 would raise about $2.4 billion.[28]

The age of Keynes, with its emphasis on protecting us from the ravages of war and depression mainly by striking a balance between consumption and employment, is on the wane. An ancient agenda, which includes our obligations to the vulnerable that Keynes acknowledged, is now forced on us: one that considers resources, population, the biosphere, and ultimately the place of humans in society and in nature. While Keynes's ideas have led to a world out of balance, we need not be buffeted from one defunct philosopher or economist to another. We have a philosophy of governance that grounds our duties to each other at home and abroad, and to our children's children, and now lets us see afresh the role of government and citizens alike as trustees of life on our sacred planet.

The trust conception of government provides an agenda that will enable all of us to stop destroying ourselves and wasting our heritage. It shows us why we must have trustees whom we can trust. It authorizes the government to help save our children from unnecessary disease, malnutrition, and ignorance; give men and women the means to have only the children they will love and can provide for; stop the slaughter on our streets; help us avoid addictions; allow us to see a doctor when we are sick; stop the world trade in the instruments of death and destruction. We are not required to keep paving over our farmland and cutting down our forests faster than they can regrow; we do not need to sacrifice our history to a perverse and inhuman idea of "progress"; we can choose not to place the biosphere at risk for a few more plastic gadgets.

A fiduciary program is financially feasible in the short run and even financially positive in the long run. It is also politically feasible because, rather than balkanizing society, it unites us around a historically grounded yet forward-looking agenda. Efforts to control guns are part of the same set of concerns that inform attempts to limit teenage pregnancy. People dedicated to arms control share the same worldview as those who would stop the destruction of our ancient forests. Those who champion educating our children can work hand in hand with those who would save our farms. We can adopt a framework for thinking about government and make common cause with each other, and even with many on the Right open to new ideas. We are not separate interest groups pushing a disjointed agenda, but men and women concerned about ourselves and each other, our children, our nation, and our planet.

The task of restoring the public trust does not rest with the voters and the public sector alone. As Keynes noted, political theorists set the underlying agenda, and for this reason philosophers must resume their social function. Over the last two decades, the Right has invested millions and millions in the development, articulation, and promotion of its *philosophy.* Those who believe that public office and public lands should not be for sale, that sustainable agriculture is more important than squeezing the last few bushels of wheat out of a parcel of land, that we should protect the vulnerable, and that parenthood is a sacred duty had better get the message very soon. Unless a *public philosophy* is set out, articulated, and promoted that is an alternative to the tragically mistaken views of the Right and the misguided views of the center, we can expect nothing more than the continued destruction of our society and the biosphere.

We need to return to the truths that our ancestors knew were self-evident: that all persons are created equal, that "usufruct"—benefiting from the earth while leaving it intact for the future—defines the relation of those people to the world, that those who lead hold a sacred trust, and that the only way that that trust can be earned is through the development and preservation of free men and women, capable of governing themselves, not through "free" markets.

1. THE SOURCES OF DISILLUSION

1. See John Palmer and Isabel Sawhill, "Perspectives on the Reagan Experiment," in their *The Reagan Experiment* (Washington, D.C.: Urban Institute, 1982), pp. 1–28.

2. David Stockman, *The Triumph of Politics* (New York: Harper & Row, 1986), pp. 181–82.

3. Charles L. Heatherly, ed., *Mandate for Leadership: Policy Management in a Conservative Administration* (Washington, D.C.: Heritage Foundation, 1981), p. iv.

4. Sidney Blumenthal, *The Rise of the Counter Establishment: From Conservative Ideology to Political Power* (New York: Times Books, 1986), pp. 45–46.

5. Gregg Easterbrook, "Ideas Move Nations," *Atlantic* (January 1986), p. 77.

6. Ibid.

7. Easterbrook lists the following antiliberal public policy groups: the Cato, Manhattan, Lehrman, Hudson, Shavano, Pacific, Sequoia, and Competitive Enterprise institutes; the committees on the Present Danger, for the Survival of a Free Congress, and for the Free World; the institutes for Foreign Policy Analysis, for Contemporary Studies, and for Humane Studies; the centers for the Study of Public Choice, for the Study of American Business, and for Judicial Studies; the Political Economy Research Center; the Reason Foundation; the Washington, American, Capital, and Mountain States legal foundations; the Ethics and Public Policy Center; the National Center for Policy Analysis; the National Institute for Public Policy; and the Washington Institute for Values in Public Policy (ibid., p. 66).

8. Ibid., p. 80.

9. It is possible to formulate a defense of the social agenda of the religious Right within a libertarian framework. For example, if the fetus is a person—a crucial assumption–then it naturally and easily follows that the fetus should be protected by the state. Libertarianism focuses on the freedom of adults, and, insofar as pornography involves children, libertarian philosophy offers it no protection from state intervention. The position of the Right on school prayer can be interpreted as increasing the liberty of parents to raise their children as they wish. Seen from this perspective, it is not a matter of forcing children to do something that they do not want to do. It is rather restoring to parents a choice that they should have had all

along. The coalitions that Reagan and Bush were able to assemble were not so artificially contrived after all.

10. *Cato Policy Report* 13, no. 1 (January/February 1991): 1.

11. Edward H. Crane, "Private Property and Perestroika," *Cato Policy Report* 13, no. 1 (January/February 1991): 13.

12. Robert Kuttner, "Inside the Democratic Think Tanks: What's the Big Idea?" *New Republic* (18 November 1985), p. 23.

13. Ibid.

14. For example, in his introduction to Arthur Okun's *Equality and Efficiency: The Big Tradeoff* (Washington, D.C.: Brookings, 1975), then Brookings president Kermit Gordon writes, "The tone and character of the book . . . distinguish it from most Brookings publications. It is a personal work, recording the author's values, judgments and experience." The feature of the book that made it an exception to the canon was that it contained an explicit discussion of rights and other values.

15. See Donald T. Critchlow, *The Brookings Institution, 1916–1952* (Dekalb: Northern Illinois University Press, 1985), p. 4.

16. Ibid., p. 9. It is reasonable to assume that "the Republic" refers both to the American republic and to Plato's *Republic*, which was supposed to be governed by an elite.

17. There are at least two reasons for doubting that this way of stating the fact/value distinction holds up. One is that administrative roles have a great deal of discretion built into them. Authorizing legislation typically carries a rather vague mandate. There is no way to decide what to do without making value judgments. Second, the distinction overlooks the role that administrative agencies play in the value-shaping process. Reports and testimony from administrative agencies help set the value agenda of elected officials.

18. Critchlow, *The Brookings Institution*, pp. 60–61. A dispute over objectivity and the role of value had already occurred in 1927 between Walton Hamilton and Moulton: "Because certain value assumptions would be interjected into any definition of the public interest, Hamilton insisted that economics develop a broad political perspective of society. Thus Hamilton argued that the Graduate School, by emphasizing the liberal arts, which Willoughby and Brookings took for theoretical nonsense, was satisfying the primary goal of the program—the training of a cadre of economists to enter government as policy makers. Hamilton lost the debate" (p. 80). The Graduate School was one of the two institutions out of which Brookings was formed. William Willoughby, a statistician, was the head of a precursor to Brookings called the Institute for Government Research. Willoughby's selection as head of the Institute for Government Research reflected the ascendant role that political scientists would play in the efficiency and economy movement.

19. See A. J. Ayer, *Language, Truth and Logic* (New York: Dover, 1952).

20. I am indebted to Herman Daly for this point.

21. "Inside the Democratic Think Tanks," Kuttner, p. 26.

22. John Rawls, *A Theory of Justice* (Cambridge, Mass.: Harvard University Press, 1971). Two other books, neither widely read, more immediately relevant to

policy are Henry Shue's *Basic Rights* (Princeton, N.J.: Princeton University Press, 1980) and Charles Beitz's *Political Theory and International Relations* (Princeton, N.J.: Princeton University Press, 1979).

23. A parallel difficulty afflicts the historical study of political theory. As Richard Ashcraft (*Revolutionary Politics and Locke's "Two Treatises of Government"* [Princeton, N.J.: Princeton University Press, 1986]) notes,

> For many years, political theory has been conceived as a subcategory of philosophy. And as a subsidiary, it has been subject to the governing rules of its parent discipline.... Hence, interpreters are inclined to search for systematic logical relationships among the concepts contained in a work of political theory, or to extract from the latter universally valid or timeless principles, analogous to the axioms of geometry or the laws of physics, or to employ certain propositions advanced by the theorist as empirically verifiable or falsifiable hypotheses, or to take the text as a kind of private language, whose meaning is revealed by unraveling the internal connections between certain statements by the author. In other words, a particular work of political theory is assumed to make sense insofar as it can be explained or reconstructed using one or more of these philosophical approaches, although interpreters differ among themselves as to which approach best describes the enterprise of philosophy itself. (pp. 3–4)

The restrictive assumptions that plague the historical study of political theory help shape and limit our political landscape as well.

24. For a discussion of many ideas for the new Clinton/Gore administration, see, e.g., *Mandate for Change* (New York: Berkeley, 1993), edited by Will Marshall and Martin Schram of the Progressive Institute. Loosely modeled after *Mandate for Leadership*, *Mandate for Change* presents a number of principles of progressive government (opportunity, reciprocal responsibility, community, democracy, and entrepreneurial government [pp. xvi–xvii]), but no overarching theory of political legitimacy.

25. Bill Clinton and Al Gore, *Putting People First: How We Can All Change America* (New York: Times Books, 1992), p. 226.

26. Al Gore, *Earth in the Balance* (New York: Houghton Mifflin, 1992). See esp. the chapters entitled "Self-Stewardship" and "Environmentalism of the Spirit."

2. JUSTIFYING THE CONSERVATIVE REVOLUTION

1. Charles L. Heatherly, ed., *Mandate for Leadership: Policy Management in a Conservative Administration* (Washington, D.C.: Heritage Foundation, 1981).

2. Ibid., p. vii.

3. Charles L. Heatherly, ed., *Mandate for Leadership II: Policy Management in a Conservative Administration* (Washington, D.C.: Heritage Foundation, 1984).

4. Gregg Easterbrook, "Ideas Move Nations," *Atlantic* (January 1986), p. 72.

5. Heatherly, ed., *Mandate for Leadership*, pp. 959–60.

6. For a discussion of the environmental effects of this executive order, see V. Kerry Smith, ed., *Environmental Policy under Reagan's Executive Order* (Chapel Hill: University of North Carolina Press, 1984).

7. For a discussion of the various barriers to the development of freer markets, see Amitai Etzioni, *Eastern Europe: The Wealth of Lessons* (Washington, D.C.: Socio-Economic Project, 1991).

8. This distinction follows that given by Fernand Braudel in *The Wheels of Commerce* (New York: Perennial Library, 1986), pp. 223–24.

9. Milton Friedman, *Capitalism and Freedom* (Chicago: University of Chicago Press, 1982); Milton Friedman and Rose Friedman, *Free to Choose* (New York: Avon, 1979).

10. Friedrich A. von Hayek, *The Road to Serfdom* (Chicago: University of Chicago Press, 1945).

11. See *Economic Report of the President* (Washington, D.C.: U.S. Government Printing Office, 1982), esp. pp. 27–35.

12. Milton Friedman, *Free to Choose* pp. xv, xvii.

13. Michael Novak, *The American Vision: An Essay on the Future of Democratic Capitalism* (Washington, D.C.: American Enterprise Institute, 1978). p. 26.

14. See Isaiah Berlin, "Two Concepts of Liberty," in *Political Philosophy*, ed. Anthony Quinton (Oxford: Oxford University Press, 1967), pp. 141–52.

15. Friedman, *Capitalism and Freedom*, pp. 11–12.

16. Ibid., p. 13.

17. Ibid., p. 8.

18. Ibid., p. 9.

19. Ibid., p. 17.

20. Ibid., p. 21.

21. Novak, *The American Vision*, pp. 9–10.

22. Ibid., p. 9.

23. On the supply of money, see Friedman, *Capitalism and Freedom*, chap. 3, and on free international trade, chap. 4.

24. Ibid., pp. 25, 27.

25. For instance, in *Public Sector Economics* (Oxford: Basil Blackwell, 1986), C. V. Brown and P. M. Jackson define public goods as nonexcludable and/or nonrival (see esp. pp. 28–29). A good is nonexcludable, e.g., if it is not technically feasible to deny it to someone. National defense is often thought to have this property because the government cannot supply it to one person without supplying it to another. A good is considered nonrival when the marginal cost of adding another person is zero. An uncrowded bridge is a good example. Since goods can be nonrival without being nonexcludable, the class of public goods generated under this definition is vastly larger than the class generated by the definition relied on by Friedman.

26. Friedman, *Capitalism and Freedom*, p. 23.

27. Ibid., p. 30.

28. Ibid., p. 32.

29. Ibid., pp. 28, 28, 29.

30. Ibid., p. 191.

31. Karl Polanyi, *The Great Transformation* (Boston: Beacon, 1944), p. 67.

32. Ibid., p. 57.

33. For a brilliant discussion of the way in which a commercial understanding of property values justified the colonists in transforming the landscape of New England and led to the extinction of the native cultures that had flourished there for thousands of years, see William Cronin, *Changes in the Land* (New York: Hill & Wang, 1983).

34. See, e.g., George Gilder, *Wealth and Poverty* (New York: Basic, 1981).

3. WHAT'S WRONG WITH THE RIGHT

1. For an excellent study of the influence of Milton Friedman on the Reagan administration, see Elton Rayack, *Not So Free to Choose: The Political Economy of Milton Friedman and Ronald Reagan* (New York: Praeger, 1987). Rayack's chapter on the influence of the "Chicago Boys" on Chile and the Pinochet regime is especially revealing. In general, the book makes a compelling case that Friedman's handling of factual matters is far from what one would expect from a leading scientist.

2. Milton Friedman and Rose Friedman, *Free to Choose* (New York: Avon, 1979), pp. xvi–xvii.

3. Milton Friedman, *Capitalism and Freedom* (Chicago: University of Chicago Press, 1982), p. 22.

4. Friedman, *Free To Choose*, pp. xv–xvi, xxi, 17, 21.

5. Friedman, *Capitalism and Freedom*, p. 28.

6. Ibid., p. 27.

7. Ibid., p. 26.

8. Karl Polanyi, *The Great Transformation* (Boston: Beacon, 1944), p. 65.

9. Friedman, *Capitalism and Freedom*, p. 13.

10. For a defense of this view, see, e.g., John Rawls, *A Theory of Justice* (Cambridge, Mass.: Harvard University Press, 1971).

11. Friedman, *Capitalism and Freedom*, pp. 108–9, 110.

12. Ibid., pp. 110, 111.

13. Ibid., p. 13.

14. Data for this section were drawn from the following sources: George Thomas Kurian, *The New Book of World Rankings* (New York: Facts on File, 1984); *The World in Figures* (London: Economist, 1987); *The 1989 Information Please Almanac*, 42d ed. (Boston: Houghton Mifflin, 1989); U.S. Department of Commerce, *Statistical Abstract of the United States, 1989* (Washington, D.C.: U.S. Government Printing Office, 1989).

15. The bulk of the human race probably does not have the instrumentalist mentality and the concern for gain that the Right assumes are fundamental features of human nature. The Amish in the United States refer to those in the mercantile culture that surrounds them as "the English" because of this concern with gain for its own sake, whatever the ethnic origin of those involved. The use of the term is an implied criticism.

16. Friedman, *Free to Choose*, pp. 16, 19.

17. For a discussion of the way in which economics misunderstands the moral aspects of human motivation, see Amitai Etzioni, *The Moral Dimension* (New York: Free Press, 1988).

18. Charles Darwin, *The Descent of Man*, in *The Origin of Species and The Descent of Man* (New York: Modern Library, n.d.), p. 914.

19. See, e.g., Darwin's account in chap. 21 of *The Descent of Man* of how morality is possible from an evolutionary perspective. An interesting interpretation of motivation from this point of view can be found in Richard Dawkin, *The Selfish Gene* (New York: Oxford University Press, 1989). As his title suggests, Dawkin stresses the selfishness of the gene—and shows how this can lead to cooperative behavior in which individuals engage in altruism.

20. Adam Smith, *The Theory of Moral Sentiments* (London: Henry G. Bohn, 1853), p. 3.

21. The social security system, which Budget Director David Stockman was so intent on dismantling by shifting it to an actuarial basis, is one way to socialize the responsibility we all have toward our parents. The system we actually have rests on a hybrid justification. By making social security rest in part on contributions from workers, it recognizes that people have a responsibility to provide for themselves when they can. But, from the beginning, it has had an additional rationale. It was meant simply to help the aged. Franklin Roosevelt, who fashioned the current system in the mid-1930s, explained his motivation:

> I had been away during the winter time and when I came back I found that a tragedy had occurred. I had an old farm neighbor, who had been a splendid old fellow—supervisor of his town, highway commissioner of his town, one of the best of our citizens. Before I left, around Christmas time, I had seen the old man, who was eighty-nine, his old brother, who was eighty-seven, his other brother, who was eighty-five, and his kid sister, who was eighty-three....
>
> When I came back in the spring, I found that in the severe winter that followed there had been a heavy fall of snow and one of the old brothers had fallen down on his way out to the barn to milk the cow, and had perished in the snow drift.
>
> The town authorities had come along and taken the two old men and had put them in the county poorhouse, and they had taken the old lady and sent her down, for want of a better place, to the insane asylum, although she was not insane but just old.

Roosevelt is quoted in Richard E. Neustadt and Ernest R. May, *Thinking in Time* [New York: Free Press, 1986], pp. 97–98.) Roosevelt insisted on individual accounts only to keep Congress from later dismantling the system. The funds in fact come from a common pool. By not tying benefits exclusively to contributions from each individual—and by financing the difference between what people have contributed and what they get with a tax on the wages of those now working—the system recognizes the obligation that one generation has to those who bore and nurtured them, who gave them life. No civilized person denies such obligations, yet, on the voluntaristic model embraced by the Right, no such responsibilities need arise even toward one's own parents. The preindustrial world we have lost, referred to by

Friedman, where family members were responsible for the aged, has been destroyed by the rise of the market itself. Once you have a highly mobile labor force, which properly functioning markets require, the family and community bonds that once succored the aged are undercut.

22. Robert E. Goodin, *Protecting the Vulnerable* (Chicago: University of Chicago Press, 1985), p. 92.

23. The voluntaristic model does not capture everything that is at stake even in those cases in which we have made choices. The fact of choice is not necessarily fundamental. Marriage is a relationship in which some of our strongest and most important obligations and joys can arise. When we marry, we promise, typically, to assist each other in time of need. But that obligation would not be nonexistent if one's betrothed fell ill the day before the wedding, before the promise is made, rather than the day after. The moral and legal contract that is involved in marriage is a codification and reaffirmation of the deeper commitment, often unspoken in its earliest stages.

24. The distinction between liberty and the value of liberty follows Rawls (see *A Theory of Justice*, pp. 201–5).

25. These arguments about legal services and political processes are drawn from Allen Buchannan, "Deriving Welfare Rights from Libertarian Rights," in *Income Support: Conceptual and Policy Issues*, ed. Peter G. Brown et al. (Totowa, N.J.: Rowman & Littlefield, 1981), pp. 233–45.

26. These arguments about the distinctions between positive and negative rights are derived from Henry Shue, *Basic Rights* (Princeton, N.J.: Princeton University Press, 1980), chap. 2.

27. Friedman, *Capitalism and Freedom*, pp. 1–2.

28. Ibid., pp. 25, 27.

29. Friedman discusses property on pp. 58 and 127 of *Free to Choose*. Elinor Ostrum rejects both the notion that commons problems always require the imposition of a solution by the state and the idea that creating private property rights will always be the solution: "Instead of presuming that the individuals sharing a commons are inevitably caught in a trap from which they cannot escape, I argue that the capacity of individuals to extricate themselves from various types of dilemma situations *varies* from situation to situation" (*Governing the Commons: The Evolution of Institutions for Collective Action* [New York: Cambridge University Press, 1990], p. 14).

30. One of Friedman's arguments against inheritance taxes is that "the inheritance of property can be interfered with more readily than the inheritance of talent" (*Free to Choose*, p. 127). He then states that there is no *ethical* difference between the inheritance of talent and the inheritance of property. Why the fact that one can be affected more easily than the other is not an ethical difference is not explained.

31. *The Essence of Friedman*, ed. Kurt R. Leube (Stanford, Calif.: Hoover Institution Press, 1987), pp. 29–31.

32. Arguments similar to mine on this point can be found in Richard Nelson,

"Rules of Government in a Mixed Economy," *Journal of Policy Analysis and Management* 6, no. 4 (Summer 1984): 541–56.

33. See, e.g., C. V. Brown and P. M. Jackson, *Public Sector Economics* (Oxford: Basil Blackwell, 1985), pp. 27–37. Paul A. Samuelson defines a good as public when "each individual's consumption of such a good leads to no subtraction from any other individual's consumption of that good" ("The Pure Theory of Public Expenditure," *Review of Economics and Statistics* 36 [November 1954]: 387).

34. For a similar argument, see Jesse Malkin and Aaron Wildavsky, "Why the Traditional Distinction between Public and Private Goods Should Be Abandoned," *Journal of Theoretical Politics* 3, no. 4 (1991): 335–78.

35. An alternative conservative attempt to justify very limited government appeals to a theory of natural rights. Works representative of this school include Robert Nozick, *Anarchy, State and Utopia* (New York: Basic, 1974); and Richard Epstein, *Takings: Private Property and the Power of Eminent Domain* (Cambridge, Mass.: Harvard University Press, 1985). Both Epstein and Nozick misread Locke, whom they cite as an ally (see n. 1, chap. 5, below). But their treatment of externalities, e.g., is inadequate on independent grounds.

Nozick's theory relies on torts—suits for damages—to deal with cases like pollution in which one person's activities harm another. Externalities would be corrected by civil law suits, not government action. There are several problems with this approach. It creates compensable property rights in the bodies of others, thus undercutting Nozick's central claim that we have absolute control over our own bodies. The tort approach is also unable to deal with long-term hazards that would have effects for decades or beyond, given the problems of proving a causal relation between agent and harm, and given the problem that the people causing long-term problems may no longer be around to pay. These problems with accountability undercut the intended incentive effect of the tort system.

Epstein avoids these defects by explicitly allowing the state to regulate harms such as nuisances, but then denies the wide-ranging implications of this conception. He justifies undercutting much environmental regulation only by ignoring the interconnected aspects of the natural world and the effect of this interconnectedness on humans.

36. The weaknesses in Friedman's position do not stop here. Friedman's position is actually compatible with a functionally diverse state. A structural difficulty—what might be called Friedman's latent utilitarianism or majoritarianism—undercuts all his arguments. As we saw in chapter 2, Friedman seems open to some level of redistribution if enough people in society find the existence or sight of poverty upsetting. Suppose we are offended by strip mining, or high rents, or pornography, or whites in a black neighborhood. Pretty soon we will have, not a little state at all, but a new Leviathan. Friedman says that we should always assign some extra weight to the preservation of liberty, but he does not say how much liberty or how other values should be weighed. His framework thus fails to protect the very idea he says he values the most.

37. The idea that creating private property rights is a solution to environmental problems is carried to new levels of absurdity in Terry L. Anderson and Donald R. Leal, *Free Market Environmentalism* (Boulder, Colo.: Pacific Research Institute for Public Policy, 1991).

38. See, e.g., James E. Hinish, Jr., "Regulatory Reform: An Overview," in *Mandate for Leadership: Policy Management in a Conservative Administration*, ed. Charles L. Heatherly (Washington, D.C.: Heritage Foundation, 1981), pp. 697–707, esp. p. 698.

39. Data gathered from the *Annual Report of the Director of the Administrative Office of United States Courts* (1979–90) indicate that the number of civil antitrust cases instituted by the federal government over the past two decades has declined, especially during the last decade. Interestingly, only 472 civil antitrust cases were initiated during 1990, as opposed to 1,352 in 1981.

40. Polanyi, *The Great Transformation*, pp. 79, 81.

41. Ibid., p. 102.

42. Friedrich Engels, preface to the first German edition (1845), in *The Condition of the Working-Class in England; from Personal Observation and Authentic Sources* (Moscow: Progress, 1980), p. 13.

43. Engels describes the slums as a place "in which the filth and tottering ruin surpass all description. Scarcely a whole window-pane can be found, the walls are crumbling, door-posts and window-frames loose and broken, doors of old boards nailed together, or altogether wanting in this thieves' quarter, where no doors are needed, there being nothing to steal. Heaps of garbage and ashes lie in all directions, and the foul liquids emptied before the doors gather in stinking pools. Here live the poorest of the poor, the worst paid workers with thieves and the victims of prostitution indiscriminately huddled together, the majority Irish, or of Irish extraction, and those who have not yet sunk in the whirlpool of moral ruin which surrounds them, sinking daily deeper, losing daily more and more of their power to resist the demoralizing influence of want, filth, and evil surroundings" (Friedrich Engels, *The Conditions of the Working Class in England in 1844* [London: George Allen & Unwin, 1892], p. 27).

44. See ibid., pp. 144–45.

45. "The great mortality among children of the working-class, and especially among those of the factory operatives, is proof enough of the unwholesome conditions under which they pass their first years.... The result in the most favorable case is a tendency to disease, or some check in development, and consequently less than normal vigour of the constitution. A nine year old child of a factory operative that has grown up in want, privation, and changing conditions, in cold and damp with insufficient clothing and unwholesome dwellings, is far from having the working force of a child brought up under healthier conditions. At nine years of age it is sent into the mill to work 6.5 hours . . . until the thirteenth year; then twelve hours until the eighteenth year" (ibid., p. 150).

46. Ibid., p. 265.

47. See ibid., p. 266.

48. Many such regulations were in place even before Engels published *The Conditions of the Working-Class* in 1845.

49. Polyani, *The Great Transformation*, p. 131.

4. THE FAILURE OF MARKET FAILURES

1. Many of the ideas contained in this chapter also appeared in my "The Failure of Market Failures," *Journal of Socio-Economics* 21, no. 1 (Spring 1992): 1–24.

2. Edith Stokey and Richard Zeckhauser, *A Primer for Policy Analysis* (New York: Norton, 1978), pp. 257, 293.

3. John Stuart Mill, *Utilitarianism*, in *The English Philosophers from Bacon to Mill* (New York: Modern Library, 1939), p. 900.

4. These three criticisms are found in John Rawls, *A Theory of Justice* (Cambridge, Mass.: Harvard University Press, 1971), pp. 22–33.

5. Jeremy Bentham, *Anarchial Fallacies: Being an Examination of the Declaration of Rights Issued during the French Revolution*, vol. 2 of *Works of Jeremy Bentham*, ed. John Bowring (New York: Russell & Russell, 1962), art. II, p. 501.

6. See Stokey and Zeckhauser, *Primer for Policy Analysis*, p. 293.

7. For a discussion of the problems of discounting, see my "Policy Analysis, Welfare Economics, and the Greenhouse Effect," *Journal of Public Policy and Management* 7, no. 3 (Spring 1988): 471–75.

8. Foreign nationals are either at risk when their well-being conflicts with our national interest, ignored, or assumed to be protected by their own governments. An administration's attitude toward noncitizens will depend on its (usually implicit) view about international relations. In my judgment, failure to resolve, and to some degree even recognize, these issues at the conceptual level explains a good deal of the instability in our foreign policy. For a provocative discussion of standing, see Duncan MacRae and Dale Whittington, "The Issue of Standing in Cost/Benefit Analysis," *Journal of Public Policy Analysis and Management* 5, no. 4 (Summer 1986): 665–82.

9. To anyone acquainted with the history of ethics, the endorsement of *individually* oriented utility-maximizing behavior must come as a shock. Although welfare economics is one of the progeny of utilitarianism, the conception of responsibilities toward others is altogether different. This is Mill without altruism. For Mill, the proper standard of individual conduct was not to maximize personal utility but to maximize utility generally: "The creed which accepts as the foundation of morals utility, or the greatest happiness principle, holds that actions are right in proportion as they tend to promote happiness, wrong as they tend to produce the reverse of happiness." One should not show favoritism toward oneself: "The greatest happiness principle . . . is a mere form if words are without rational signification, unless one person's happiness, supposed equal in degree (with the proper allowance made

for kind), is counted for exactly as much as another's (Mill, *Utilitarianism*, pp. 900, 946).

10. Walter Nicholson, *Intermediate Microeconomics and Its Application* (Chicago, Dryden, 1983), p. 519.

11. See Derek Parfit, "Energy Policy and the Further Future: The Social Discount Rate," in *Energy and the Future*, ed. Douglas MacLean and Peter G. Brown (Totowa, N.J.: Rowman & Littlefield, 1983), pp. 31–37.

12. John McPhee, *Basin and Range* (New York: Farrar, Straus & Giroux, 1980), p. 129. The distinction between animal and deep time is borrowed from this volume.

13. Reference to William Nordhaus, "How Fast Should We Graze the Global Commons," *American Economic Review: Papers and Proceedings* 72, no. 2 (May 1982): 242–46 as an example of the neoclassical conception.

14. See Lynn White, Jr., "The Historical Roots of Our Ecological Crisis," *Science* 155, no. 3767 (10 March 1967): 1203–7.

15. In the second book of Genesis, which contains the second account of the origins of mankind, the role of "dominion . . . over the earth" is not assigned to man.

16. These points are derived in part from Keith Thomas, *Man and the Natural World* (New York: Pantheon, 1983).

17. Aldo Leopold, *A Sand County Almanac* (New York: Oxford University Press, 1966). For a discussion of the implications of the theory of evolution for the way in which we conceive of the moral community, see James Rachels, *Created from Animals: The Moral Implications of Darwinism* (New York: Oxford University Press, 1990).

18. For a discussion of how this problem of scale came to be left out and the implications of this oversight, see Herman Daly, "Elements of Environmental Macroeconomics," in *Ecological Economics: The Science and Management of Sustainability*, ed. Robert Costanza (New York: Columbia University Press, 1991), pp. 32–46.

19. Milton Friedman and Rose Friedman, *Free to Choose* (New York: Avon, 1979), p. 293.

20. A faculty member of the Kennedy School of Government, who is himself an economist, once assured me that professorships of economics *were* for sale. Fortunately, there is no evidence that this is official university policy—although it does reveal an uncritical state of mind, a fascination with the market.

21. Michael Walzer, *Spheres of Justice* (New York: Basic, 1983), p. 100.

22. For a discussion of the present state of the law on this subject, see Susan Hankin Denise, "Regulating the Sale of Human Organs," *Virginia Law Review* 71, no. 6 (September 1985): 1015–38. In general, organs may not legally be sold.

23. For Friedman's discussion of the role of the state in controlling the money supply, see *Capitalism and Freedom* (Chicago: University of Chicago Press, 1982), chap. 3, esp. p. 55.

24. See, e.g., Edward E. Zajac, "Perceived Economic Justice: The Example of Public Utility Regulation," in *Cost Allocation: Methods, Principles, Applications*, ed. H. Peyton Young (Amsterdam: Elsevier Science, 1985), pp. 119–53.

25. Ibid., p. 123.

26. Charles L. Heatherly, ed., *Mandate for Leadership: Policy Management in a Conservative Administration* (Washington, D.C.: Heritage Foundation, 1981), p. 960. It could be argued that these subsidies are attempts to control externalities that one generation might impose on another by wasting topsoil and thus correct for artificially low food prices for this generation. If we believe that we should conserve resources for the future—and most people believe that we should—it is much more effective to make this argument directly rather than be burdened with the circumlocution of "externalities."

27. Friedman, *Capitalism and Freedom*, p. 32.

28. The nonrivalness definition of public goods, relied on by economists in the utilitarian as opposed to the libertarian tradition, will not help much in legitimating what we do either. Congestion occurs easily among those who wish to view the Constitution.

29. This is how Walzer proposes thinking about the state in *Spheres of Justice*.

30. Hank C. Jenkins-Smith, *Democratic Politics and Policy Analysis* (Pacific Grove, Calif.: Brooks/Cole, 1989); and David L. Weimer and Aidan R. Vining, *Policy Analysis: Concepts and Practice* (Englewood Cliffs, N.J.: Prentice-Hall, 1989). For another example of a book that explores some of the foundations of policy analysis, see Duncan MacRae, Jr., and James Wilde, *Policy Analysis for Public Decision* (North Scituate, Mass: Duxbury, 1979).

5. THE PUBLIC TRUST

1. Both Robert Nozick (*Anarchy, State and Utopia* [New York: Basic, 1974]) and Richard Epstein (*Takings: Private Property and the Power of Eminent Domain* [Cambridge, Mass.: Harvard University Press, 1985]) claim that their theories are grounded in Locke. Neither reading is credible. Historically, they take only a portion of Locke's conception of natural rights, ignoring entirely the requirements of natural law. Besides undercutting their claims to historical authority, this partial view also commits them to all the mistakes of a voluntaristic account of obligations. They completely miss the Janus-faced aspect of contract theory: that we enter into the contract because of our vulnerability. Even in contract theory itself, it is the vulnerability, not the promise, that is foundational. In addition, in order to block redistribution, both use the argument that all actions of the state must be unanimous. But as Ian Shapiro has noted, this requirement backfires since, if some people want redistribution, the minimum state does not enjoy unanimous support either (see his *The Evolution of Rights in Liberal Theory: An Essay in Critical Anthropology* [Cambridge: Cambridge University Press, 1986], p. 163).

There is a symmetry in the inadequacies of contemporary theories of the state. Those on the Right, such as Nozick's and Epstein's, fail to provide any account of the duties of the rich. Those on the Left, like John Rawls's as set out in *A Theory of*

Justice (Cambridge, Mass.: Harvard University Press, 1971), fail to provide any account of the obligations of the poor. The trustee conception grounds the obligations of both.

2. For a discussion of the widespread use of this concept before and subsequent to Locke, see J. W. Gough, "Political Trusteeship," in his *John Locke's Political Philosophy* (Oxford: Clarendon, 1973), pp. 154–92. For a discussion of human trustworthiness in Locke's thought, see John Dunn, "The Concept of 'Trust' in the Politics of John Locke," in *Philosophy in History*, ed. Richard Rorty et al. (Cambridge: Cambridge University Press, 1984), pp. 279–301.

3. *Second Treatise* (*ST*) par. 156. All quotations of Locke's *Second Treatise* are taken from *The English Philosophers from Bacon to Mill*, ed. Edwin A. Burtt (New York: Modern Library, 1939), pp. 403–503.

4. *ST*, pars. 123, 124, 131.

5. Bernard Bailyn, *The Ideological Origins of the American Revolution* (Cambridge, Mass.: Harvard University Press, 1967), p. 30. Of course there is controversy about Locke's role, but note John Diggin's comment: "The extent to which John Locke influenced Jefferson and other American Founders is a subject of controversy among contemporary historians.... Ironically, however, the Loyalists of the eighteenth century wanted to deny Locke's attitudes not only because they were erroneous but because they were ubiquitous" (John Patrick Diggins, *The Lost Soul of American Politics* [New York: Basic, 1984], p. 32).

6. This account of the duties of the trustee is taken, with modifications, from *Putting the Public Trust Doctrine to Work*, prepared by David C. Slade (Washington, D.C.: Coastal States Association, 1990).

7. *ST*, par. 7.

8. Locke advances both theological and naturalistic arguments in favor of the idea that everyone counts. Theologically, each person is a creation of God and valuable for that reason. But Locke also claims that persons in the state of nature "should be equal one amongst another without subordination or subjection" (*ST*, par. 4).

9. John Locke, *A Letter Concerning Toleration*, in *Locke on Politics, Religion, and Education* (New York: Collier, 1965), pp. 104–46.

10. *ST*, par. 222.

11. Locke's conception of rights roughly tracks with the tripartite cluster of rights that Henry Shue sets out in *Basic Rights* (Princeton, N.J.: Princeton University Press, 1980).

12. *ST*, pars. 22, 27.

13. Locke is ambivalent on how much is owed the poor, although he says over and over again that persons with substantial property may not deny food and other necessities to those in need. See, e.g., *ST*, par. 183: "He that hath and to spare must remit something of his full satisfaction, and give way to the pressing and preferable title of those who are in danger to perish without it."

14. *ST*, par. 129.

15. *ST*, par. 27.

16. See Edith Brown Weiss, "The Planetary Trust: Conservation and Intergenerational Equity," *Ecology Law Quarterly* 2, no. 4 (1984): 495–581.

17. Quoted in Richard Ashcraft, *Revolutionary Politics and Locke's "Two Treatises of Government"* (Princeton, N.J.: Princeton University Press, 1986), p. 266.

18. Here I follow Weiss, "The Planetary Trust," pp. 512–16.

19. *ST*, par. 34.

20. *ST*, par. 37 (added in later editions).

21. Ashcraft, *Revolutionary Politics*, p. 266.

22. *ST*, par. 38.

23. I am indebted to Robert Sprinkle's discussion of realism in *Profession of Conscience: The Making and Meaning of Life-Sciences Liberalism* (Princeton, N.J.: Princeton University Press, in press).

24. Thucydides, *The Peloponnesian War* (New York: Random House, 1951), p. 331. (emphasis added).

25. *ST*, par. 175.

26. See, e.g., *A Short Guide to Clausewitz on War*, ed. Roger Ashley Leonard (New York: Capricorn, 1968), p. 57.

27. For a discussion of the principles of just warfare, see, e.g., Michael Walzer, *Just and Unjust Wars* (New York: Basic, 1977).

28. *ST*, par. 26.

29. Gen. 1:26 (Revised English Bible). Lynn White has suggested that the concept of *dominion* has done much to legitimate the destruction of the natural world (see Lynn White, Jr., "The Historical Roots of Our Ecological Crisis," *Science* 155, no. 3767 [10 March 1967]: 1203–7, but this overlooks the responsibilities that go with a proper understanding of power or dominion.

30. Charles Darwin, *The Descent of Man*, in *The Origin of Species and The Descent of Man* (New York: Modern Library, n.d.), p. 920. Interestingly, a revision in the conception of the moral community to which we belong does seem to have been under way well before Darwin. It does not, however, reach as far back as Locke. As Keith Thomas notes (*Man and the Natural World* [New York: Pantheon, 1983], pp. 242–43),

> At the start of the early modern period, man's ascendency over the natural world was the unquestioned object of human endeavor. By 1800 it was still the aim of most people and one, moreover, which at least seemed firmly within reach. But by this time the objective was no longer unquestioned. Doubts and hesitations had arisen about man's place in nature and his relationship to other species. The detached study of natural history had discredited many of the early man-centred perceptions. A closer sense of affinity with the animal creation had weakened old assumptions about human uniqueness. A new concern for the sufferings of animals had arisen; and, instead of continuing to destroy the forests and uproot all plants lacking practical value, an increasing number of people had begun to plant trees and to cultivate flowers for emotional satisfaction.
>
> These developments were but aspects of a much wider reversal in the relationship of the English to the natural world. They were part of a whole complex of changes which, in the later eighteenth century, had helped to overthrow many established assumptions and create new sensibilities of a kind that have gained in intensity ever since.

31. Aldo Leopold, *A Sand County Almanac* (New York: Oxford University Press, 1966), p. 240.

32. See Michael Walzer, *Spheres of Justice* (New York: Basic, 1983), p. 7.

33. As Walzer puts it, "Money seeps across all boundaries—this is the primary form of illegal immigration" (ibid., p. 22).

34. The simply appalling behavior of many lawyers who justify deception on the ground that the lawyer is to further the interests of the client fails to recognize that attorneys are also officers of the court and thus have obligations to preserve the integrity of judicial processes.

35. See Edmund Burke, *Reflections on the Revolution in France* (Indianapolis: Hackett, 1987).

36. Julian L. Simon, *The Ultimate Resource* (Princeton, N.J.: Princeton University Press, 1981), pp. 3–11.

37. For figures on malnourishment, see *World Resources, 1990–1*, ed. Allen L. Hammond (New York: Oxford University Press, 1990), p. 8; on water shortages, pp. 6, 161–78; and on air pollution, pp. 8, 201–16. In the chapter "Food and Agriculture," the following "mixed picture" is presented: (1) many of the gains from the Green Revolution have already occurred; (2) many regions have little potential for increasing cropland, and that under use is stressed to maintain current production practices; and (3) "the number of undernourished people has increased in absolute terms but has probably declined in percentage terms in most regions" (p. 84).

38. This relies on Robert E. Goodin, *Protecting the Vulnerable* (Chicago: University of Chicago Press, 1985), p. 110.

39. I am indebted to Robert Sprinkle for this point.

40. I am indebted to David Rodgers for these points.

41. For an account of the virtues present in a liberal account of the state, see William A. Galston, *Liberal Purposes: Goods, Virtues, and Diversity in the Liberal State* (Cambridge: Cambridge University Press, 1991).

42. This is far preferable to the onerous duties in classical utilitarianism, which makes us responsible for the happiness of all persons—far too strong a set of obligations to make it possible to preserve our own purposes and projects and thus incompatible with a moral and religious life. (This is brilliantly argued by Bernard Williams in his "Critique of Utilitarianism," in *Utilitarianism: For and Against*, by J. J. C. Smart and Bernard J. Williams [Cambridge: Cambridge University Press, 1973], pp. 75–155. It is also preferable to Friedman's account, according to which we have *no* obligations to others, an ethic that flies in the face of the fundamentals of the Judeo-Christian tradition. Welfare economics is still stuck with the principle of utility, along with too strong a requirement of altruism, but dodges it in practice by means of the idea of the invisible hand and by not having any principle of distribution. The trustee doctrine steers a nice middle course between these two implausible accounts of our duties to noncompatriots.

43. See Henry David Thoreau, *Walden and Civil Disobedience* (Boston: Riverside, 1957), pp. 231–56.

44. The requirement to preserve all persons could seem to lead to distortions in another direction. How much should we spend to preserve someone? In an age of increasingly sophisticated medical technology, it could seem that trusteeship requires us to spend limitless amounts merely to keep people alive, a problem particularly acute with respect to the elderly. But the conception of the person as chooser and goal setter can help keep expenditures in line. We are obligated to keep alive only those people capable of exercising choice. Recognizing death as brain death keeps the requirement to preserve all persons from being an open-ended authorization to spend money.

6. RESTORING GOVERNMENT AND PRESERVING PERSONS

1. Total PAC contributions were only $32 million in 1980. (All these figures come from the testimony of Fred Wertheimer, president of Common Cause before the House Task Force on Campaign Finance Reform, 28 May 1991, p. 4.

2. The "Common Cause Campaign Finance Background Paper: Soft Money" (Washington, D.C.: Common Cause, May 1990) states, "The Bush and Dukakis campaigns reportedly raised more than $20 million each in political party soft money" (p. 1).

3. I am indebted to Ethan Brown for pointing this out to me.

4. National Commission on Children, *Beyond Rhetoric: A New American Agenda for Children and Families* (Washington, D.C.: U.S. Government Printing Office, 1991), p. xviii.

5. Children's Defense Fund, *Leave No Child Behind* (Washington, D.C.: Children's Defense Fund, 1991), p. 5.

6. For a discussion of the literature on what to do about our children and our families, see William Galston, "Home Alone," *New Republic* (2 December 1991), pp. 40–44.

7. These figures come from National Commission on Children, *Beyond Rhetoric*, p. 151.

8. For a critical review of the WIC program for not taking into account the fact that many of the health problems of poor mothers and their children are behavioral, not nutritional, see George G. Graham, "WIC: A Food Program That Fails," *Public Interest*, no. 103 (Spring 1991): 66–75.

9. These figures come from National Commission on Children, *Beyond Rhetoric*, p. 191.

10. For a discussion of reforms needed in Head Start, see Douglas J. Besharov, "New Directions for Head Start," *The World and I*, June 1992, pp. 515–20.

11. For a comprehensive bibliography, see *An Annotated Bibliography of the Head Start Research since 1965* (Washington, D.C.: U.S. Government Printing Office, 1985, June).

12. Families who do not owe that much in taxes would receive a payment equal to the difference between the amount they would otherwise owe and $1,000. Thus,

a family with one child that would otherwise owe $340 would receive a check for $660 instead.

13. See *A Call for Action: The Pepper Commission: U.S. Bipartisan Commission on Comprehensive Health Care* (Washington, D.C.: U.S. Government Printing Office, 1990).

14. Henry J. Aaron, *Serious and Unstable Condition: Financing America's Health Care* (Washington, D.C.: Brookings, 1991), p. 151. The plan is outlined on pp. 140–52.

15. The data in this paragraph are taken from "Handgun Facts" and "Handgun Laws in Other Industrialized Countries," supplied by Handgun Control (Washington, D.C.).

16. This idea was suggested to me by Albert Bowker.

17. A City of St. Louis program that successfully purchased over 7,000 guns is described in the *New York Times* (20 November 1991), p. B1.

18. For a discussion of how capitalism tends to undermine its own moral foundations, see Daniel Bell, *The Cultural Contradictions of Capitalism* (New York: Basic, 1976).

19. Job training is an essential government function if citizens are to be protected from economic hardship.

20. For a discussion of the role of the liberal state in maintaining a core set of values through education, see William Galtson, *Liberal Purposes* (Cambridge: Cambridge University Press, 1991).

21. In 1982, there were 3.7 million births, of which an estimated 1.3 million resulted from unintended pregnancies, and approximately 1.6 million induced abortions (Jaqueline Darrouch Forrest, "Unintended Pregnancy among American Women," *Family Planning Perspectives* 19, no. 2 [March/April 1987]: 76–77).

22. Elise F. Jones et al., "Unintended Pregnancy, Contraceptive Practice and Family Planning Services in Developed Countries," *Family Planning Perspectives* 20, no. 2 (March/April 1988): 67.

23. The New York City public school system began distributing free condoms to all high school students on 26 November 1991.

24. As of 1992, four research centers for contraception and infertility have been established. Two contraception centers have been established, one at the University of Virginia and one at the University of Connecticut. Two infertility centers have been established, one at the University of Michigan and one at Massachusetts General Hospital.

25. Testimony of Health and Human Services secretary Louis W. Sullivan before the Senate (see U.S. Senate Committee on Labor and Human Resources, *Tobacco Product Education and Health Protection Act of 1990, Part 1*, S. hrg. 107–707, pt. 1. 101st Cong., 2d sess., 20 February 1990 [Washington, D.C.: U.S. Government Printing Office, 1990], pp. 18–38, 21, 22.

26. *The Health Consequences of Smoking: Nicotine Addiction: A Report of the Surgeon General* (Rockville, Md.: U.S. Department of Health and Human Services, Public Health Service, Centers for Disease Control, Center for Health Promotion

and Education, Office of Smoking and Health, 1988), p. 9. (This document is available through the U.S. Government Printing Office, Washinton, D.C., as SuDoc.HE 20.7614:988.

27. Testimony of Louis Sullivan, p. 22.

28. *Health United States, 1989* (Hyattsville, Md.: U.S. Department of Health and Human Services, 1990), pp. 70, 123.

29. On 11 December 1991, the *Wall Street Journal* reported that "three surveys published in today's Journal of the American Medical Association found that the ads for Camel cigarettes featuring the animated Joe Camel mascot are highly effective in reaching children" (p. B1).

30. Additional steps that should be pursued with respect to tobacco have been developed and endorsed by the American Cancer Society, the American Heart Association, and the American Lung Association. Their proposals should become federal law. Tobacco products should come under health and safety laws such as the Consumer Product Safety Act. There should be a well-enforced federal law that makes it illegal to sell tobacco products to anyone under twenty-one years of age. The promotion of tobacco products through free samples, coupons, or discounts should be prohibited, as should their sale through vending machines. All advertisements of tobacco products in association with sports events should be banned. For similar reasons, alcohol advertising at sporting events should be prohibited.

31. See "Tobacco Aid," *Common Cause Magazine* (March/April 1991), p. 9.

32. As energy prices rise, the ability to move food vast distances at very low costs will decrease, and a more regionally oriented agriculture will emerge (for the reasons set out in chapter 7 and according to the schedule set out in chapter 8). Land now used for tobacco in the South can thus be converted to the production of vegetables and dairy products to serve the adjacent markets in the cities and towns of the region. In some cases, especially on steeper slopes or near streams, reforestation may be the best option and would have been far preferable to farming in the first place.

33. For a statement of a way to restructure foreign assistance to take into account the collapse of the Soviet Empire, see John W. Sewell and Peter M. Storm, *United States Budget for a New World Order* (Washington, D.C.: Overseas Development Council, 1991).

34. See, e.g., Nicholas D. Kristof, "Stark Data on Women: 100 Million Are Missing," *New York Times* 5 November 1991), pp. C1, C12.

35. Shue argues that the only way to ensure that subsistence and bodily rights are guaranteed *as* rights is to have governments that are accountable. A benign dictatorship that provides for the subsistence of its citizens does not do so *as* a right (Henry Shue, *Basic Rights* [Princeton, N.J.: Princeton University Press, 1980], p. 76).

36. Gross domestic product (GDP) and a cluster of other indicators are widely taken to be measures of economic well-being. The fortunes of our elected leaders, our own, are closely connected to these indicators. Yet there are a number of reasons for thinking that these indicators are misleading.

First, GDP is not a measure of economic benefits, as is widely supposed. Rather, it is a measure of benefits *and costs*. Natural disasters will appear in GDP because of the economic costs of the recovery effort, but the events often represent a severe loss of well-being. Similar problems arise in relation to disasters of human origin like oil spills, attempts to protect ourselves against urban air pollution, and the like. Hence, GDP can, and often does, rise while well-being is falling.

Second, GDP does not measure natural resource depletion and hence does not provide reliable evidence of whether any given level of economic activity can be sustained because of limitations of inputs. Cutting the old-growth forests in the Pacific Northwest shows up positively in the indicators but, above certain rates of sustainability, undercuts long-term economic and other dimensions of well-being. Income can rise while the ability to sustain it falls.

Third, GDP does not provide any measure of the degree of inequality of income. It can and does rise while poverty increases.

Fourth, GDP provides no measure of the carrying capacity of the biosphere on which all economic activity depends. It is indifferent to scale. This includes the issue of resource depletion mentioned above, but goes beyond it in two respects. (i) We have to be concerned with the sinks—disposal sites—for the by-products of economic activity. With respect to at least two sinks, we seem to have exceeded the carrying capacity of the earth at this time: carbon dioxide with resulting climate change and chlorofluorcarbons (CFCs) and the loss of stratospheric ozone. But the problem is quite general. (ii) GDP measures only human well-being and thus gives no indication of whether the total level of economic activity is compatible with the well-being of nonhuman animals and plants. GDP can rise, at least temporarily, while the health of the biosphere declines.

37. For a discussion of this point of view, see Martha C. Nussbaum and Amaryta Sen, eds., *The Quality of Life* (Oxford: Clarendon, 1993). For an excellent summary of this school of thought, see David Crocker, "Functioning and Capability: The Foundations of Sen's and Nussbaum's Development Ethic," *Political Theory* 20, no. 4 (November 1992):584–612.

38. The Rocky Mountain Institute, Snowmass, Colorado, has an extensive literature on this subject.

39. For a discussion of the way environmental regulations can spur innovation and economic growth, see Alan S. Miller, "Cleaning the Air While Filling Corporate Coffers: Technology Forcing and Economic Growth," *Annual Survey of American Law* (New York University School of Law), no. 1 (1990): 69–82.

40. Memorandum from the UN General Assembly, Preparatory Committee for the UN Conference on Environment and Development (New York, 19 July 1991), p. 12.

41. New Jersey has a provision in its 1992 welfare law that denies extra benefits to women who have additional children while on welfare (see *New York Times* [18 January 1992], p. 25).

42. William W. Kaufmann and John D. Steinbruner, *Decisions for Defense: Prospects for a New Order* (Washington, D.C.: Brookings, 1991), p. 75–76, 68.

43. John Mueller, *Retreat from Doomsday* (New York: Basic, 1989), p. 264.

44. According to the 1992 United Nations report of the UN High Commissioner for Refugees (E/1992/59), there were more than 17 million refugees worldwide in 1991, a large proportion of whom had been displaced by war.

45. *SIPRI Yearbook, 1991* (Oxford: Oxford University Press, 1991), p. 198.

46. This might require an armed international force with ships, planes, and troops that could enforce these prohibitions. In case of UN inaction, a default mechanism could come into play, whereby a regional security force could be used. A critical component of this strategy would be a strengthened and much better enforced nonproliferation treaty to stop the spread of nuclear weapons and the use of inspections where it is believed that countries have the scientific and technical capabilities to build nuclear weapons despite current restrictions on the availability of their design and components.

7. HOW TO STOP WASTING OUR CHILDREN'S HERITAGE

1. In *Earth in the Balance* (New York: Houghton Mifflin, 1992), Al Gore has recommended what he calls a global Marshall Plan, one consisting of five elements: the stabilization of the world population; creation of appropriate technologies; changing economic accounting to include ecological consequences; new international agreements to enforce conservation of the biosphere; and an international education program to educate all the world's citizens about the global environment. The fiduciary conception provides the philosophical foundation for such a plan.

2. For an excellent discussion of the attitudes of various religions toward nature, see Steven C. Rockefeller and John C. Elder, eds., *Spirit and Nature* (Boston: Beacon, 1992).

3. While the United States is responsible for almost 20 percent of the carbon dioxide introduced into the earth's atmosphere each year, it has only 5 percent of the world's population. For why the problem of the greenhouse effect cannot be analyzed in the framework of neoclassical economics and why attempts to do so by economists like William Nordhaus and Thomas Schelling may be legitimating inaction for fallacious reasons, see my "Climate Change and the Planetary Trust," *Energy Policy* 20, no. 3 (March 1992): 208–22.

4. Joel B. Smith and Dennis A. Tirpak, eds., "The Potential Effects of Global Climate Change on the United States" (draft report to Congress) (Washington, D.C.: U.S. Environmental Protection Agency, 1988), p. 49.

5. The rise will result from the interaction of three separate causes. First, less water may be held in the form of snow, ice caps, and glaciers. There is likely to be more water in the oceans, although for a period this could be offset by increased snowfall. Because warmer air holds more moisture, some glaciers may grow. Second, the water will be hotter, and hotter water takes up more space owing to thermal expansion. Third, the plate on which the East Coast of the United States rests is

gradually sinking. This subsidence is not related to the greenhouse effect, but it adds to greenhouse-induced changes.

6. For a discussion of the effects of climate change on biodiversity, see *World Resources, 1990–1* (New York: Oxford University Press, 1990), pp. 130–34.

7. Even those who hold that the effects of climate change are likely to be benign argue in favor of at least slowing the rate of change as a precautionary measure to protect against sudden and unexpected changes in weather patterns and, thereby, world agriculture.

8. In *Energy Use in the Greenhouse* (El Cerrito, Calif.: International Project for Sustainable Energy Paths, September 1989), Florentin Krause, Wilfred Bach, and Jon Koomey have estimated that to hold the temperature rise to about one-tenth of one degree per decade between now and the year 2100 we will have to restrict total emissions to 300 billion tons of carbon during that period. This emissions budget assumes the simultaneous implementation of other steps, such as eliminating chlorofluorocarbons (CFCs) and increasing the amount of carbon stored in the world's forests. Such a combined strategy could require the following emission reduction milestones: a return to 1985 levels by the year 2005, to 20 percent below those levels by 2015, to 50 percent below them by 2030, and to 75 percent below them by 2050.

9. For a discussion of the allocation issues in stabilizing global climate, see H. Peyton Young and Amanda Wolf, "Global Warming Negotiations: Does Fairness Matter?" *Brookings Review* 10 (Spring 1992), p. 2–8.

10. Julian Simon, *The Ultimate Resource* (Princeton, N.J.: Princeton University Press, 1981).

11. For a summary of the limitations on expanding agricultural output, see Pierre R. Crosson, "Sustainable Agriculture," *Resources* no. 110 (Winter 1992): 14–17.

12. Herman Daly, "Elements of Environmental Macroeconomics," in *Ecological Economics: The Science and Management of Sustainability,* ed. Robert Costanza (New York: Columbia University Press, 1991), pp. 32–46.

13. For a far-ranging discussion of biodiversity, see E. O. Wilson, ed., *Biodiversity* (Washington, D.C.: National Academy Press, 1988).

14. Bouvier assumes that, over the next century, overall health will improve and that, in 2080, life expectancy will reach eighty-eight years. One effect of this increased longevity will be an increased percentage of older people in the population. An increasingly aged population will of course necessitate periodic restructuring of the social security system, possibly pushing back the age at which benefits can begin and making benefits fully taxable. Since these changes will be phased in over a long period of time, people will have time to adjust their expectations accordingly. For more detail on this scenario, see Leon F. Bouvier, "How to Get There from Here: The Demographic Route to Optimal Population Size," in *The NPG Forum* (Teaneck, N.J.: Negative Population Growth, 1989).

15. Senator Henry Jackson, with the backing of the Nixon administration, proposed a bill outlining a national land use policy in January 1970. That bill was, however, at least in part, one of the casualties of Watergate because administration

support declined sharply when John Ehrlichman, chairman of the Domestic Council and a key supporter of the legislation, resigned. The fate of this legislation is discussed by Sidney Plotkin in "Policy Fragmentation and Capitalist Reform: The Defeat of National Land-Use Policy," *Politics and Society* 9, no. 4 (1980): 409–45. I am grateful to James Cohen for pointing this out to me.

16. See John DeGrove, "Managing Growth in Other States: A National Perspective" (paper presented at the conference "Balanced Growth: Promoting the Economy and Protecting the Environment," University of Maryland at College Park, October 1991).

17. According to DeGrove (ibid.), a study of housing costs in Oregon has shown that the establishment of urban growth boundaries has not caused housing prices to rise.

18. See Bryan Norton, "Ecological Health and Sustainable Resource Management," in *Ecological Economics*.

19. John A. Humbach, "Law and a New Land Ethic," *Minnesota Law Review* 74, no. 227 (1989): 339–70. p. 370.

20. See *Lucas v. South Carolina Coastal Council*, 119 L. Ed. 2d 561, 112 S. Ct. 2935 (1992).

21. We can outflank those who object to regulation in the name of extreme property rights by making eligibility for public services dependent on compliance with the state land use plan. Perhaps the simplest way to do this is to refuse to allow property owners who do not comply access to public roads: no compliance would mean no driveway permit. This leaves the landowner with all his putative "rights" intact and brings into very sharp focus the role of public investment in creating property values.

22. Information on the Ramsar convention can be obtained from the International Waterfowl Research Bureau, Slimbridge, Gloucestershire, GL2 7BK England.

23. For discussion of the restoration of aquatic ecosystems, see *Restoration of Aquatic Ecosystems: Science, Technology, and Public Policy* (Washington, D.C.: National Research Council, 1991).

24. These principles are discussed in Daly, "Elements of Environmental Macroeconomics," pp. 44–45. With respect to nonrenewable resources, Daly writes, "Receipts from the exploitation of a nonrenewable resource should be divided into an income component and a capital component. The division is made such that by the end of the life expectancy of the nonrenewable asset, a new renewable asset will have been built up by the annual investment of the capital component. The annual sustainable yield from that renewable asset must be equal to the income component of the nonrenewable asset that is being consumed annually from the beginning" (p. 45).

25. National Heritage Conservation Act, 101st Cong. 2d sess., 1990. S. Doc. 3105.2.

26. For a study that makes at least implicit use of the fiduciary conception, see,

e.g., William R. Cline, *The Economics of Global Warming* (Washington, D.C.: International Institute of Economics, 1992).

27. For a discussion of the ways in which trade undercuts biodiversity, see Richard B. Norgaard, "The Rise of the Global Exchange Economy and the Loss of Biological Diversity," in Wilson, ed., *Biodiversity*, pp. 206–11.

28. John Audley suggested this idea to me.

29. For an exceptionally insightful discussion of a comprehensive package outlining a program of sustainable development, see *Compact for a New World* (Washington, D.C.: World Resources Institute, 1991).

8. PAYING FOR A SUSTAINABLE, RESPONSIBLE SOCIETY

1. The figures and the plan that follow come from *House of Representatives Campaign Spending Limit and Election Reform Act of 1991*, H. Rept. 102-340, pt. 1 (Washington, D.C.: U.S. Government Printing Office, 1991), esp. pp. 64, 66.

2. The figures and the plan that follow come from *Senate Elections Ethics Act of 1991: Report of the Committee on Rules and Administration*, S. Rept. 102-37 (Washington, D.C.: U.S. Government Printing Office, 1991), p. 44.

3. Owen M. Fiss, "Why the State?" in *Democracy and the Mass Media*, ed. Judith Lichtenberg (Cambridge: Cambridge University Press, 1990), p. 137.

4. For a discussion of the behavior of the Reagan administration in this respect, see Fiss, "Why the State," pp. 137–38. Fiss correctly points out that what is at stake are fundamental issues of state legitimacy.

5. For a discussion of three regulatory models for mass communication, see Henry Geller, "Mass Communications Policy: Where We Are and Where We Should Be Going," in Lichtenberg, ed., *Democracy and the Mass Media*, pp. 290–330. On the second ground for a return to the fairness doctrine, see esp. pp. 293–310.

6. Fiss, "Why the State," p. 152.

7. Henry J. Aaron, *Serious and Unstable Condition: Financing America's Health care* (Washington, D.C.: Brookings, 1991), p. 146.

8. *A Call for Action: The Pepper Commission: U.S. Bipartisan Commission on Comprehensive Health Care* (Washington, D.C.: U.S. Government Printing Office, 1990), pp. 270, 275.

9. *Current Housing Problems and Possible Federal Response* (Washington, D.C.: Congressional Budget Office, 1988), p. 106. This volume discusses a number of other approaches to housing assistance.

10. These estimates were made with the assistance of Carla Pedone of the Congressional Budget Office.

11. These figures are taken from Michael Isikoff, "200 Million Guns Reported in Circulation Nationwide," *Washington Post* (24 May 1991), p. A1. Isikoff's figures are taken from Bureau of Alcohol, Tobacco, and Firearms data.

12. William W. Kaufman and John D. Steinbruner, *Decisions for Defense: Prospects for a New Order* (Washington, D.C.: Brookings, 1991), p. 74.

13. John W. Sewell and Peter M. Storm, *United States Budget for a New World Order* (Washington, D.C.: Overseas Development Council, 1991).

14. For the figures reported here and more on the Development Assistance Committee, see *1991 Report: Development Co-operation* (Paris: Organization for Economic Co-operation and Development, 1991), esp. pp. 12, 171.

15. For a discussion of the confusion that now surrounds the concept of sustainable development, see, e.g., Sharachchandra M. Lele, "Sustainable Development: A Critical Review," *World Development* 19, no. 6 (1991): 607–21.

16. *Meeting the Population Challenge* (New York: UN Population Fund, n.d.), p. 9.

17. Ibid., pp. 11, 42.

18. *1990 Report on Progress toward Population Stabilization* (Washington, D.C.: Population Crisis Committee, 1990).

19. The figures in this section are taken from *Selected Spending and Revenue Options* (Washington, D.C.: Congressional Budget Office, 1991), pp. 163–64.

20. Milton Russell, E. William Colglazier, and Mary R. English, *Hazardous Waste Remediation: The Task Ahead* (Knoxville: University of Tennessee Press, 1991), p. 12.

21. This figure is taken from a misguided attempt to analyze the issues raised by the Endangered Species Act in terms of cost/benefit trade-offs by Charles C. Mann and Mark L. Plummer ("The Butterfly Problem," *Atlantic* [January 1992], p. 52). This article is a good example of the sort of reasoning that currently characterizes much of the policy debate. In addition to failing to notice that not everything can be or is distributed in accordance with market criteria, four other steps are usually involved. Step 1 is to find some large number to cite. Step 2 is to ignore, or mention only in passing, any direct benefits that might accrue from the action in question. Step 3 is to ignore any indirect benefits, such as employment, that might be associated with government expenditures in implementing the policy in question. Step 4 is to claim that one could not seriously consider spending the amount cited in step 1 on the task in question. On the basis of the figures that Mann and Plummer cite—and characterize as impossibly out of reach—it would cost each American about $1.75 a year to save all endangered species in the United States.

22. This figure is taken from Paul F. O'Connell, "Sustainable Agriculture," in *Agriculture and the Environment* (Washington, D.C.: U.S. Government Printing Office, 1991), p. 177. For a definition of sustainable agriculture and its policy implications, see Rod J. MacRae et al., "Policies, Programs, and Regulations to Support a Transition to Sustainable Agriculture in Canada," *American Journal of Alternative Agriculture* 5, no. 2 (1990): 76–92. See also *Sustainable Agriculture Research and Education in the Field* (Washington, D.C.: National Research Council, 1991).

23. See Florentin Krause, *The Role of Carbon Taxes in Strategies to Reduce Fossil Carbon Emissions* (El Cerrito, Calif.: International Project for Sustainable Energy Paths, 1992), p. 7.

24. The figures in this paragraph have been supplied by Florentin Krause.

25. For a discussion of severance taxes, see Talbot Page, *Conservation and Economic Efficiency: An Approach to Materials Policy* (Baltimore: Johns Hopkins University Press, 1977).

26. See C. V. Brown, *Taxation and the Incentive to Work* (New York: Oxford University Press, 1983).

27. See Philip Stevens, "Tax Cuts Do Not Spur Employees to Work Harder," *Financial Times* (16 December 1986).

28. National Commission on Children, "Beyond Rhetoric: A New American Agenda for Children and Families (Washington, D.C.: U.S. Government Printing Office, 1991), pp. 377, 380.

Weimer, David, *Policy Analysis* (with A. Vining), 66
Weiss, Edith Brown, 74
Well-being of persons, trust conception of, 71–72
Wetlands, protecting, 121, 126
Women, Infants, and Children (WIC) program, 96, 133
Work incentives, progressive taxes and, 139–40

"World Heritage Sites," 121
World War I, 48
World War II, 28, 50, 76

Zajac, Edward, 59
Zeckhauser, Richard, *A Primer for Policy Analysis* (with E. Stokey), 50, 51, 53, 54
Zones, proposed types of, for land, 119